Portability and style in Ada®

Portability and style in Ada

Edited by

JOHN NISSEN

GEC Telecommunications Ltd, Coventry

PETER WALLIS

School of Mathematics, University of Bath

The right of the University of Cambridge to print and sell all manner of books was granted by Henry VIII in 1534. The University has printed and published continuously since 1584.

Published on behalf of
the Commission of the European Communities by
CAMBRIDGE UNIVERSITY PRESS
Cambridge
London New York New Rochelle
Melbourne Sydney

Published by the Press Syndicate of the University of Cambridge
The Pitt Building, Trumpington Street, Cambridge CB2 1RP
32 East 57th Street, New York, NY 10022, USA
296 Beaconsfield Parade, Middle Park, Melbourne 3206, Australia

First published 1984

Printed in Great Britain at the University Press, Cambridge

Library of Congress catalogue card number:

British Library cataloguing in publication data

Nissen, John
Portability and style in Ada.-(Ada companion series)
1. Ada (Computer program language)
I. Title   II. Wallis, Peter
001.64'24   QA76.73.A35

ISBN 0 521 26482 0

Contents

Preface

This book contains two guides, one on portability of Ada programs and one on Ada programming style. These guides were produced by the Ada-Europe Portability Working Group, set up in December 1980 under the chairmanship of John Nissen. Meetings of the Ada-Europe working groups are partially funded by the Commission of the European Communities. The Commission has supported the publication of the guides. An early version of the Portability Guide was published as an NPL report, and we are grateful for NPL's permission to publish a revised version in this book.

In the question of portability an well as style there is considerable judgement to be exercised. Reference to the rules might be made in a contract. Every care has been taken to ensure correctness; however, no liability of any kind is accepted by the authors of this book, their associated organizations, or the publisher.

Production of the guides has had to rely on a great deal of voluntary effort. The main contributors, listed as authors, were John Barnes, Bernard Dautrevaux, Ted Dowling, Stephen Goldsack, Hans Jeanrond, Trevor Moreton, John Nissen, Ron Pierce, Mario Refice, Peter Reid, Sven Tafvelin, Peter Wallis, Tim White and Brian Wichmann. Peter Wallis acted as secretary to the working group; Brian Wichmann dealt with word processing for the portability guide; John Nissen and Stephen Goldsack dealt with word processing for the style guide and index. Contributions and helpful comments have been received from other members of Ada-Europe and from elsewhere. The authors would like to thank all the people who have helped in the production of this book, and the Commission who have supported meetings of the working group. Acknowledgement should also be made of the support of the authors by their own organizations:

The General Electric Company of England, p.l.c.

SPL International

BNI, France

Ferranti Computer Systems Ltd

Imperial College

ESG Eletronik-System-GmbH

Software Sciences Ltd

University of Bari

University of York

Chalmers University of Technology

University of Bath

RSRE, UK Ministry of Defence

NPL (National Physical Laboratory, UK)

Both guides have been designed to be read in conjunction with the Ada Language Reference Manual (ANSI / MIL STD 1815 A, 1983). Therefore the section numbering follows the manual as closely as possible, and referencing is by section number rather than page number, as in the manual. There is a minimum of cross-referencing between the guides. A section number refers to the same guide unless preceded either by the name of the other guide or by "LRM" (when refering to the manual).

The guides, by their nature, can never be considered complete. The working group would welcome comments on the guides. Written comments, dated, with the author's name, address and telephone number, and quoting guide and section number, should be sent to the chairman:

John C.D. Nissen (Ada-Europe)
Section EM 862,
GEC Telecommunications Ltd,
PO Box 53,
COVENTRY, CV3 1HJ
UK

PORTABILITY GUIDE

1 Introduction

1.1 The need for Standards

Previous efforts to standardize on languages have come too late in the language life-cycle for as much program portability to be achieved as possible. For many popular languages it is not easy to write portable software, due to the variety of compiler implementations and target-machine dependencies in the language. With Ada it is possible to isolate machine dependent parts. The strictness of Ada compiler validation, and avoidance of subsetting or supersetting of the language, should reduce the effect of compilers on portability. However, the compiler-writer is given some options and expected to exercise judgement. Some constructs of the language may be implemented more or less efficiently (in space, and/or run-time) leading to the possibility of surprises to the unwary programmer. The compiler writer is expected to base some decisions as to choice of options, on the target machine. The United States Department of Defense (DoD) used to accept that some subsetting of Ada might arise due to reasonable restrictions of the target machine, e.g. absence of floating point hardware, but compilers must recognize full Ada syntax and flag use of any features not supported on the target.

Reliability is linked with portability; long-term reliability cannot be achieved if a program behaves differently after being transported to a new target. As the pace of hardware technological development increases and the proportion of software cost increases, one should aim for the software life to be longer than that of the target machine. While software is being developed, it is common to use a host for the bulk of testing. This testing is inadequate if the programs behave differently after being transported from host to target.

Reliability is also linked to portability in more subtle ways. Consider integers and ranges. Integer size is machine dependent (or, more strictly, compiler dependent). Use of ranges not only gives more portability but also more reliability because of the extra checking possible and, not to be neglected, the extra thought required by the programmer. The value of the ranges may also help another programmer to understand the purpose of the variables. Thus one has more programmer portability, i.e. ease of movement of programmers from one programming project to another. Programs are also easier to maintain giving a longer potential lifetime as well as higher reliability.

Any Ada constructs whose use affects reliability but not portability are not directly addressed by this guide.

1.2 Definition of Portability

In this guide portability is considered as a qualitative judgement on how easy it is to change a given program such that it can be recompiled by a different compiler and then run with the required behaviour, generally on a different target.

A perfectly portable Ada program would, without *any* change, be compilable by any valid Ada compiler within any Ada Program Support Environment (APSE) on any host, and be subsequently executable, with the required behaviour on the corresponding target for that compiler. In real-time applications it is rare for a program to be completely portable, because of timing considerations.

A useful measure of portability is the fraction:

$$1 - \frac{\text{cost of re-implementation on new target}}{\text{cost of original implementation}}$$

Adopting a readable and consistent style of Ada programming, together with suitable accompanying documentation, can help reduce the cost of re-implementation. However these issues are not addressed by this guide but are raised in the style guide. Note that certain applications may need to use special features of targets in order to achieve sufficient accuracy, security, availability or integrity, thus leading to programs with some inherently non-portable components.

1.2 Definition of Portability

1.3 The Approach to Portability

This guide proposes a set of rules which might be taken into account for several purposes, e.g. advice for programmers and implementors, possible basis for contractual requirements, etc. Therefore the approach has been not so much rigorous as pragmatic in the sense that most people reading this guide should be able to apply the rules.

In producing the rules a certain amount of judgement has been necessary. The rules need to be simple both to apply and to check for, without being too restrictive. At the same time a balance needs to be kept between making too many assumptions about implementations and too few. If too few are made, one is again liable to be unduly restrictive on the programmer, while not making the program significantly more portable.

Heavy emphasis is given to the use of packages to increase the portability of a program by encapsulating machine dependencies, see Chapter 7.

1.4 Structure of this Guide

This guide is intended to be read in conjunction with the Ada Language Reference Manual [ANSI 1983] hereafter referred to as the LRM. Therefore the layout and section numbering follows the manual as closely as possible. However some portability issues could be raised in a number of possible places. The earliest position has been used to avoid too much information being concentrated in the later chapters. For example, issues on floating point are raised in 3.5 rather than 13.7. We hope this will also reduce the amount of cross-reference required by the typical reader.

Each section of the LRM is considered in turn. The guide gives a series of recommendations or rules to aid portability. In any particular situation, it will be a matter of judgement as to how rigidly these rules are followed. To help in making these decisions, the rules are classified according to their importance as judged by the authors.

Those responsible for procuring Ada software may be able to use this guide in specifying the degree of portability to be achieved by the software. The classification of the rules can be used in this specification, for instance, by requiring that no mandatory rule is broken.

The classification of each of the rules and notes is as follows:

Mandatory: It is essential when using this language feature to follow the rule given.

Recommended: There are circumstances when the rule given can be broken, but never without a justification being recorded in the program.

Suggested: A suggestion to aid portability; particularly important if the text is likely to be changed.

Aid: A mechanical aid or test procedures (not necessarily currently available or even planned) that could be provided, e.g. as an APSE tool.

Information from implementors: This can be considered as supplementary to Appendix F of the LRM. Implementors may include information on target, host, compiler and APSE implementations (where a program is compiled on a host by a compiler within an APSE and the compiled code is subsequently run on a target). Corresponding to information from implementors, the characteristics of implementation required for a program should be documented with the program, e.g. whether it requires at least 32 bits for INTEGER.

Target Requirements: Characteristics of the target system required to run the program that should be documented with the program.

Note: Further information relevant to portability, or explanation of rules, aids, etc.

A guide of this nature can never be considered complete. Suggestions for improvement are welcome.

1.4 Structure of this Guide

1.5 Global Assumptions

In any programming language design, there are certain areas in which different implementations are free to assign different numerical values to certain quantities, such as the maximum number of bits available to represent an integer. The following global assumptions are made in the guide.

Any target implementation is expected to have:

1. At least 16 bits available for type INTEGER, see 3.5.4,

2. At least 6 decimal digits available for the predefined type FLOAT

3. At least 10 decimal digits available for programmer-defined floating point types, see 3.5.7,

4. At least 32-bit accuracy available for fixed-point types, see 3.5.9,

5. At least 80 character positions per line for text output on peripheral devices, see 14.3.

Any host is expected to have:

6. At least 80 characters per line of source text, see 2.2,

7. The extended character set available for source text, see 2.5,

8. At least 64-bits for universal_integer, see 4.10,

Some further assumptions may become necessary in the light of experience with Ada implementations.

1.6 Classification of Errors

The LRM defines two classes of incorrect programs which can cause problems with portability. One class is the *erroneous* category and the other is the *incorrect order dependence* category. A compiler is not required to determine if a program belongs to these two classes, but if this detection is performed, the compiler can take actions which will vary from system to system. In practice, programs which are in these two classes are using obscure features of the language which cannot be recommended.

1.6 Classification of Errors

2

Lexical elements

2.1 Character Set

A host on which a program is compiled might not include either a peripheral for printing the program written using the extended character set or a conversion aid for converting the program into an equivalent program using only the basic character set. However restriction to the basic character set is considered undesirable for legibility, and it is assumed that all hosts will support the extended set. For input-output of characters, see 14.3.

The vertical bar and sharp or number sign characters of the basic character set are reserved for national use in the ISO Standard(646), hence the rule below.

Suggested: An exclamation mark should be used in place of a vertical bar, and colon in place of the sharp or number sign in based numbers.

Aid: Converter from extended to basic character set. (An editor should suffice.)

Information from implementors: Whether listing of programs with the extended character set is possible. (This may depend upon the terminal/peripheral in use which is system dependent.)

2.2 Lexical Elements, Separators, and Delimiters

Not more than 80 character positions on a line should be used. This number has been chosen for compatibility with typical current display devices.

A horizontal tabulate is equivalent to a space between lexical units, but could affect line length and hence printability of the program on a host.

Mandatory: No control characters (known in the LRM as non-graphic characters) should be used except newline or the equivalent pair carriage-return/line-feed.

Not more than 80 character positions on a line should be used. (This may not be controlled by the implementor.)

Information from implementors: Any restriction below 80 characters per line.

Aid: Converter to remove tabs and form feeds and replace with spaces and carriage-return/line-feed equivalents appropriately.

Note: The meaning of the word "line" in the LRM is open to interpretation. It could either mean an actual line, as displayed, or a virtual line, as some internal representation of an indefinitely long sequence of characters terminated by a separator. If the former view is taken, line length is a portability issue affecting lexical units, see 2.3 and 2.4. If the latter view is taken, the implementation must provide a facility for splitting a virtual line into actual lines for display. When such splitting is unacceptable there is again a portability issue.

2.3 Identifiers

Identifiers are restricted to 80 characters by the rule of 2.2 above.

2.3 Identifiers

2.4 Numeric Literals

Numeric literals are restricted to 80 characters by the rule of 2.2 above. See 3.5.4 and 3.5.6 below.

2.5 Character Literals

Permitting all of the 95 ISO graphic characters forces APSE/host implementors to support the extended character set (or to be in 1-1 correspondence with it), see 2.1 above.

2.6 String Literals

See 2.5 concerning the characters used and also 6.7 below, about overloading "&".

2.8 Pragmas

Certain pragmas need not be recognized or acted upon by a compiler. Rules about language defined pragmas occur under the section corresponding to the LRM definition.

Mandatory: Implementation defined pragmas must not be used.

Note: The misspelling or misplacement of a pragma identifier could lead to the pragma being ignored without warning.

2.10 Allowable Replacements of Characters

Aid: An aid would be useful for replacement of vertical bar characters by exclamation marks or vice versa, sharp characters of a based literal by colons or vice versa, quotation characters by per cent characters or vice versa.

Information from implementors: Any limitation on the use of the above characters, or change in their visual representation (eg sharp character represented by £).

3
Declarations and types

3.2.1 Object Declarations

Programs which depend upon the use of uninitialized variables are erroneous. In general, the order of evaluation of default expressions is not defined by the language, and side effects in their evaluation could thus lead to incorrect order dependence.

Mandatory: Initialize variables with a value on declaration unless it can be proved that the variable is initialized before use.

The evaluation of default expressions in an object declaration must not have side effects on values in other expressions in the same declaration.

3.5 Scalar Types

Range checks are not applied to the result of every subexpression of an expression. It is possible that a subexpression could have a value outside the range specified for its type. For instance, the result of an operation on an object of an integer type T may be in the range of the parent predefined type but not within the constraint defined in the integer type definition of T. As a consequence, a subexpression may cause NUMERIC_ERROR (as opposed to CONSTRAINT_ERROR) on one particular machine but not on another. For example if a type T and a variable V are declared by

```
type T is new INTEGER range -50 .. 50;
V : T := 40;
```

then

```
V := (V + 100) - 3 * V;
```

is a valid assignment statement in Ada but it is not necessarily portable. If, on one target T is implemented as derived from a predefined type SHORT_INTEGER whose values fit into an 8-bit byte then the subexpression (V + 100) will overflow, possibly causing NUMERIC_ERROR. If on another target, T is implemented as derived from the predefined INTEGER the subexpressions may not cause any trouble. It is possible to overcome the problem by ensuring that no expression may contain more than one operator.

The language does not define the order of evaluation of the bounds. Side effects of functions for the bounds could introduce an incorrect order dependence (see 1.6 and 6.5).

Mandatory: No assumption must be made about the order of evaluation of the bounds in a range constraint.

Aid: An aid would be useful to detect the subexpressions of a scalar type which can potentially violate a declared range constraint.

3.5.4 Integer Types

Since the range of values of the predefined integer types, and also the largest available integer range are machine dependent, portability issues naturally arise. It is assumed that all targets allow at least 16 bits for the predefined type INTEGER.

Mandatory: Values of type INTEGER must lie within the range -32767 .. 32767 with corresponding ranges for NATURAL and POSITIVE. Integer ranges outside the range -32767 .. 32767 must not be used except to define new integer types.

The type-names SHORT_INTEGER and LONG_INTEGER must not be used explicitly.

Recommended: New integer types should be introduced for logically separate purposes, especially if large ranges of values are required. No integer type with a range larger than -32767 .. 32767 should be declared.

3.5.4 Integer Types

Suggested: Use of integer ranges in excess of 16 bits should be avoided unless the application demands it.

3.5.6 Real Types

Real types are either floating or fixed point types. Different remarks apply to each class.

Mandatory: Values of the type outside the range of safe numbers should not be assumed.

Recommended: The raising of the exception NUMERIC_ERROR should not be relied upon.

3.5.7 Floating Point Types

A few implementations of Ada may not support floating point efficiently because the target machine has no hardware support for floating point. It is assumed that all target machines offer at least 6 decimal digits of precision for the predefined type FLOAT.

Mandatory: A floating point constraint in excess of 6 digits should only be used to define new floating point types.

The predefined types SHORT_FLOAT and LONG_FLOAT must not be used explicitly.

Recommended: New floating point types should be introduced for logically separate purposes, especially if high accuracy is required.

Do not assume that any floating point type exists with an accuracy in excess of 10 digits.

Suggested: Use of floating point types with an accuracy in excess of six digits should be avoided. For small scale approximate computation, consider the use of fixed point. A range constraint can be included with a floating point type definition to ensure that values outside the range of safe numbers are not used. Avoid the use of inequalities which could depend upon the actual accuracy implemented rather than the requested accuracy.

Do not assume that an implementation will take any advantage of an accuracy constraint on a subtype.

Aid: The accuracy of a floating point quantity may exceed that requested. It is advisable to check the performance of an algorithm using only the requested accuracy, and an aid would be useful.

Note: It is difficult to ensure that a non-trivial floating point algorithm is numerically stable and requires only the properties of floating point guaranteed by the type definition.

3.5.8 Operations of Floating Point Types

Recommended: Avoid the use of the attributes FIRST and LAST unless an explicit range constraint is given with the corresponding type or subtype.

Information from implementors: Precisions and ranges of SHORT_FLOAT, FLOAT and LONG_FLOAT, if implemented.

Note: Control convergence by use of attributes rather than by the use of explicit constants. For example, the series A(N) + A(N+1) + A(N+2) ..., if convergent and all terms are positive, is summed by the loop

```
SUM := A(N);
J := N + 1;
while A(J) > SUM * F'EPSILON loop
   SUM := SUM + A(J);
   J := J + 1;
```

3.5.8 Operations of Floating Point Types

```
        end loop;
```

which automatically terminates when no further accuracy can be obtained. The above loop utilizes the accuracy provided by the model numbers of the type F, and hence may be expected to provide broadly the same accuracy on all targets. To obtain the accuracy of the model numbers of the base type instead, use F'BASE'EPSILON for F'EPSILON; to obtain the maximum possible accuracy on a given target outside the range of Ada model numbers, use the properties of safe number of F. In particular, computations in the range -F'SAFE_LARGE .. F'SAFE_LARGE are safe.

3.5.9 Fixed Point Types

Mandatory: A program should not, in general, depend upon a specific value for F'SMALL since an implementation is free to choose any value for this which is less than or equal to F'DELTA.

Recommended: High accuracy should not be used unless the application demands it. In particular, an accuracy which requires more than 32 bits for the model numbers should be avoided. (32 bits is the largest accuracy likely to be supported on small machines).

Aid: The accuracy of fixed point types is very critical in many applications. (With floating point, more bits are typically available and the automatic standardization improves the effective accuracy). A tool might be used to ensure that an algorithm only depends upon the properties of the fixed point type guaranteed by the type definition.

Note: A specific value for F'SMALL must be set using a representation clause if the model numbers of a fixed point type are to be the same on all machines.

3.5.10 Operations of Fixed Point Types

Mandatory: The attributes SMALL, MANTISSA and LARGE should be used only in a manner consistent with the property that F'DELTA >= F'SMALL.

Recommended: The attributes FIRST and LAST should not be used because, in general, their values are not model numbers.

3.6 Array Types

In the elaboration of a constrained array definition, the evaluation of each discrete range and the elaboration of the component subtype indication are performed in some order not defined by the language. Side effects can produce an incorrect order dependence (see 1.6 and 6.5).

Array bounds and string bounds are subject to the rules for integers and positive numbers respectively, see 3.5.4.

Mandatory: No assumption must be made about the order of evaluation of each discrete range of the index constraint, or of any component subtype indication or of the bounds in a multi-dimensional array.

3.6.1 Index Constraints and Discrete Ranges

If a discrete range is expressed with integer literals and no type name is given, type INTEGER is taken. This could make a discrete range valid on one machine but not on another (if the literals are outside the INTEGER range supported by some machine).

Recommended: Constrained types should be used for integer discrete ranges, especially if a large range is required, see 3.5.4.

3.6.1 Index Constraints and Discrete Ranges

3.7.1 Discriminants

The variable on the left hand side of an assignment statement and the expression on the right hand side may be evaluated in either order. This leads to the possibility of incorrect order dependence (see 5.2). But there is also the possibility of an erroneous program if a discriminant of a subcomponent of the variable is changed. By the same principle, if the actual parameter of a subprogram or entry call is a component that depends on discriminants of an unconstrained record variable, then the execution of the call is erroneous if the value of any discriminant of the variable is changed by this execution (see LRM 6.2).

For the elaboration of a discriminant constraint, the expressions given in the discriminant associations are evaluated in some order that is not defined by the language (see LRM 3.7.2).

Mandatory: Evaluation of an expression in an assignment, or execution of a subprogram or entry call, must not have any side effect on any discriminant in the same statement.

Evaluation of an expression of a discriminant association must not have any side effects on variables of other expressions in the discriminant constraint.

4

Names and expressions

4.1.1 Indexed Components

In certain cases one or more expressions have to be evaluated in order to evaluate a name (indexed component of a multi-dimensional name). Furthermore, the prefix part of an indexed component can be a function returning an array to be indexed.

Mandatory: A function as a prefix of an indexed component must not change an index of the same component as a side effect.

A function in an expression of an indexed component must not change the prefix or on another index of the same component as a side effect.

Note: See section 6.5

4.1.2 Slices

Mandatory: No assumption must be made about the order of evaluation of the name, prefix and discrete range of a slice.

4.1.4 Attributes

See sections 3.5.8 and 3.5.10.

4.3 Aggregates

The language does not define the order of evaluation of the expressions of the different component associations in aggregates.

Mandatory: Evaluation of expressions in component associations in aggregates must not have side-effects affecting variables appearing in other components of the same aggregate.

4.5 Operators and Expression Evaluation

The language does not define the order of evaluation of the two operands of a dyadic operator (excepting short circuit control forms).

Mandatory: The evaluation of operands (excepting operands of short circuit control forms) must not have side effects affecting other operands in the same expression.

Note: See Section 6.5.

4.5.7 Accuracy of Operations with Real Operands

Mandatory: Unless the numbers correspond exactly to model numbers, then the result of equality or inequality between floating point numbers should not be relied upon.

Note: There are cases where two differently derived numbers, theoretically equal, may be unequal in practice and vice versa. Equality/inequality of floating point numbers is especially dangerous for terminating loops.

Other rules to observe for these operations are noted in section 3.5.6.

4.6 Type Conversions

Conversions to and from real types are covered by the rules in section 4.6 of the LRM which must be observed to maintain portability.

4.6 Type Conversions

Note: The value obtained from INTEGER(X) where

X : FLOAT := 1.5 is not defined.

4.8 Allocators

Dynamic allocation should be treated with caution. Unpredictable amounts of processing power and time may be required to create an object at run-time and later to reclaim the storage occupied. Further uncertainties arise over the amount of storage taken by the object and over the moment at which the reclamation, known as deallocation and colloquially called garbage collection, takes place. Thus particular care is needed with programs in which time or storage is critical. A program which runs satisfactorily on one machine may raise the STORAGE_ERROR exception on a different machine. Specification of the size of the collection of objects can help to avoid this situation. Limiting the reclamation to the moment when the object becomes inaccessible further helps. The use of explicit deallocation (the predefined generic library procedure UNCHECKED_DEALLOCATION, section 13.10.1 of LRM) may be useful to make a program run in a limited memory. Furthermore explicit control over when deallocation takes place may be necessary in real-time programs. However, unchecked deallocation should be used with care, see the notes.

Do not attempt to access an object for which storage deallocation has been indirectly requested (by executing a FREE procedure on another pointer to the same object). The affect is not defined by the language, and the access is erroneous (see LRM 13.10.1).

Mandatory: No attempt should ever be made to access an object for which storage may be deallocated.

Recommended: The collection size should be specified if possible by using T'STORAGE_SIZE expressed in terms of the SIZE of the object of the access type, divided by SYSTEM.STORAGE_UNIT. However, due allowance should be made for the space required by the allocator for tables and links, etc (see LRM 13.2).

Information from implementors: Whether the pragma CONTROLLED is recognized and has the requested effect.

If not, when automatic storage reclamation can take place.

Whether storage is always reclaimed when an object becomes inaccessible and, if so, how soon afterwards.

The strategy for allocation of storage to dynamic arrays and records with variants.

Note: The danger of explicit deallocation is apparent from LRM 13.10.1: "If X and Y designate the same object, then accessing this object through Y is erroneous if this access is performed (or attempted) after the call FREE(X); the effect of each such access is not defined by the language." Thus a program may run satisfactorily on one machine and apparently satisfactorily on another while producing different results; alternatively the program could fail on the second machine. The LRM does not specify when the storage occupied by X (and accessed through Y) is reclaimed following a call of FREE(X). The LRM demands only that the value of X is null.

Deallocation may take place some time after the scope is left, e.g. as part of a total garbage collection process when free storage has run out. This could lead to significant hiccups in real-time processing. The programmer is given some control over deallocation by the pragma CONTROLLED and the predefined generic library procedure UNCHECKED_DEALLOCATION, each of which has been discussed.

An example of collection size specification is given in LRM 13.2 examples. The difficulty with dynamic arrays and records with variants is mentioned in LRM 13.2 notes.

4.8 Allocators

4.9 Static Expressions and Static Subtypes

Mandatory: It must not be assumed that a real static expression is evaluated with greater accuracy than that of the target machine.

4.10 Universal Expressions

Mandatory: The potential raising of NUMERIC_ERROR must be avoided by ensuring that real computations (of type universal real) are bounded in absolute value. In principle, such bounds can be exceeded but it would be wise to compute values no larger in magnitude than the largest supported value on execution. This value is about 10.0 ** (4*MAX_DIGITS). Corresponding limits for integer computation is MIN_INT..MAX_INT. In the case of literal values, one can assume MAX_DIGITS >= 10 and at least 64-bit for the type Universal integer.

5

Statements

5.2 Assignment Statement

Assignments V := E are legal where V is the name of an object and E is an expression of the same type. V may, however, be a component of a more complex structure, and its identification may involve an evaluation. It is laid down by the language definition that no element of the variable V may be changed before the expression E has been fully evaluated. However, any evaluation involved in the selection of the left-hand side and the evaluation of the expression on the right may occur in either order, or concurrently. A program has an incorrect order dependence if it relies on the order of these evaluations. It may be erroneous if a discriminant is changed (see 3.7.1).

Mandatory: Assignments in which the evaluation of the right hand expression can change the evaluation on the left or vice versa must be avoided.

Notes: Examples of erroneous programs are those where the right-hand expression involves the function which modifies, by side effects, variables appearing in the left-hand side or vice versa. These could be an index to an array, or an access variable, or a record with variants. Particular attention should be given to any statement in which the left-hand side is not a simple name, and the right-hand side involves evaluation of a function, for example:

```
A.all := F( ... );
B(N)  := F( ... );
R.D   := F( ... );
```

to ensure that the function does not have undesirable

side effects.

The third example could involve a record field which exists only for one variant of the record type. The side effect could change the variant by assignment to the record.

5.5 Loop Statements

A "for loop" is controlled by a discrete range. If the type of the control variable is not given, but the range is given in terms of integer literals, type INTEGER is assumed. For example

```
for J in 1 .. 100_000 loop
    .....
```

It is possible for such a range to be valid on one machine but not on another, see 3.5.4.

Recommended: Constrained types should always be used for integer ranges.

Notes: See also index constraints and discrete ranges 3.6.1.

6

Subprograms

6.2 Formal Parameter Modes

The language does not define whether parameters of an array, record, or private type are passed by reference or by copying. The execution of a program is erroneous if its effect depends on which mechanism is selected by the implementation. Changing a discriminant can also lead to an erroneous program (see 3.7.1).

Mandatory: If there is any possibility of sharing between a global variable and an actual parameter of an array, record, or private type, all assignments to the quantity concerned within the subprogram must be via the formal parameter.

No assumption should be made about the value of an actual parameter of array, record, or private type if the execution of the subprogram is abnormally terminated by an exception.

6.3 Subprogram Bodies

Mandatory: No assumptions should be made about whether the pragma INLINE actually has any effect.

Information from implementors: Circumstances under which the pragma INLINE is acted upon.

6.4.1 Parameter Associations

The order of evaluation of actual parameters is not defined, nor is the order of copying back "in out" or "out" parameters defined.

Mandatory: Programs must not use parameters which have side effects influencing other parameters of the same subprogram, see 6.5.

Values passed to or returned from a subprogram must be defined, except that this cannot be expected for values returned after an exception (see 6.2).

6.5 Function Subprograms

A function returns a value. The computation of such a value may involve executing a code body which accesses variables not local to the function. If the function modifies such non-local variables, the effect is called a side-effect. Functions with side effects are not forbidden entirely, since they are convenient for the implementation of certain package bodies with local protected data. However they can be the cause of many portability problems and should be used with great care. In general where an expression uses both a function value, and a variable which is modified by that function, it is undetermined whether the value of the variable before or after the function execution is to be used.

Mandatory: Functions with side effects must not be used in circumstances which cause sensitivity to the order of evaluation.

Note: The following program is not portable since the component of A selected could be A(3, 1) or A(3, 2).

```
declare
   J : INTEGER := 1;
   A : array (1 .. 3, 1 .. 3) of .... ;
   function F return INTEGER is
   begin
      J := J + 1;
      return 3;
   end;
begin
   A(F, J) := ... ;
end;
```

6.7 Overloading of Operators

The overloading of the operator "&" could cause naive Ada source ode handlers (such as prettyprinters) to produce misleading results in reformatting strings.

Recommended: Additional overloadings for the operator "&" on character types should not be defined.

7

Packages

Packages provide the main mechanism for modularising Ada programs. Hence they should be used whenever possible to encapsulate machine dependencies. The principle is that any part of the program that has to be machine-dependent should be 'hidden' from the bulk of a portable program by encapsulating it inside a package body. If all the versions of such a package for different machines can be used in exactly the same way, then when the program is moved to another machine the package itself must be rewritten but no rewriting is necessary of those parts of the program that use the package.

Some care is needed to relate this overall requirement to more detailed requirements for packages containing machine-dependent code. If a package simply provides procedures with machine-independent specifications and machine-dependent bodies, that package can be written with a machine-independent specification and a machine-dependent body. However, a choice is available for the writing of packages that provide access to machine-dependent constants. The values of such constants can be provided to the program by supplying them by function calls (in which case the package has a machine-independent specification and a machine-dependent body, as before); alternatively the constant values can be set within the package specification for direct use by the rest of the program. The second alternative may lead to more efficient generated code, but has the disadvantage that the package specification needs changing when the program is moved to another machine. Note that whichever method is used no changes to the program using the package are necessary beyond those to the package specifications.

Because of the central importance of packages for portable Ada programming, it is considered mandatory to report through comments the portability characteristics of packages.

Mandatory: A comment at the beginning of each package must clearly state the portability characteristics both of its specification and of its body. If values of constants set in the specification are machine-dependent they must be clearly described to facilitate the calculation of the appropriate values for another target. If parts of the body need rewriting for a different target, this must be clearly stated and some guidance to the necessary rewriting given.

Recommended: Packages with adequate and preferably proven portability should be used whenever possible.

If programs are required with similar function but different performance, e.g. different efficiency, space/time behaviour, portability or reliability characteristics, then the parts of the programs that must differ should be encapsulated by packages whose bodies differ.

8
Visibility rules

The rules for scoping and visibility contained in LRM Chapter 8 do not affect portability. However some restrictions should be observed.

8.5 Renaming Declarations

Renaming can affect clarity, etc. but not portability directly. However, it is worthwhile including the following rule.

Recommended: Renaming should not be used to change the name of any entity from the package STANDARD (see LRM Appendix C), or machine-dependent values from the package SYSTEM. This ensures that the use of any such machine-dependent values in the user's program remains obvious.

Aid: A source code auditor would be useful to check that no undesirable renaming takes place.

9 Tasks

A program that uses tasking may suffer from significant portability problems because instruction execution times vary from machine to machine. This will affect both the relative execution times of tasks and their individual absolute execution times. In some cases a program may not be capable of running at all on a particular machine lacking the required processing power.

An ideal implementation would provide an infinitely fast processor for each task. In practice not only will a processor take a finite time but it may need to deal with a number of tasks according to some scheduling algorithm. Differences in the scheduling algorithm are also likely to hinder portability. Thus we cannot expect a program to have identical real-time behaviour on different machines and so our notion of portability must be somewhat weakened. This section therefore is largely concerned with avoiding the writing of programs whose behaviour is grossly discontinuous with respect to execution times. As an example a program may appear to work on a particular machine despite the uncoordinated use of shared variables merely because of fortuitous timing. Such a program is clearly not portable. On the other hand a program which correctly provides various accesses to a structure such as a buffer using the rendezvous mechanism will also behave differently on different machines, for example the queue lengths may vary in a slightly different way and so some events may occur in a different order; however the overall behaviour could be deemed portable. Note furthermore that global optimization may have a dramatic effect on task timings and therefore on portability.

A target machine may comprise a number of processing units. The machine's run-time support may allow a task to run on any of a number of processing units, according to availability and perhaps suitability. It is expected that the rendezvous and timing mechanisms will behave essentially as on a multiprogrammed, single processing unit machine, at least as far as the Ada application program is concerned. However a task may actually execute in parallel with another, even one of higher priority. For portability, a program must allow for this.

If the processing units are "loosely coupled" (i.e. not sharing high speed memory) and possibly distributed, it is expected that tasks will be allocated to processing units on a semipermanent basis, e.g. for their lifetime (barring processing unit failure). Communication can take place by rendezvous or by messages in the form of intermediate tasks created for the purpose. The rendezvous is likely to take significantly longer between separated tasks than between tasks on the same processing unit or between tasks on a tightly coupled machine (i.e. with shared high speed memory). Intermediate tasks can be created for the sole purpose of conveying information from a sending task to a receiving task in such a way as to allow the sender to continue running while the receiver is receiving and processing the information. Such intermediate (or "messenger") tasks can be coded in Ada, and run on a single processor or tightly coupled machine; but on a loosely coupled or distributed system they need to have special recognition by the compiler for implementation as messages. Standards are required for this to ensure portability of message-based programs.

Message-based programs may be written, not because of the target machine architecture, but because of the nature of the problem to be solved. If a task is to deal with a number of transactions, or similar entities, in an interleaved fashion, it may not be possible for it to be delayed while calling for a rendezvous on behalf of one of them. In this case it may send a message, allowing it to continue processing on the other entities. Ideally the task would originally be coded as if it were dealing with a single entity, and then transformed to enable it to deal with a number of entities. The transformation should preserve correctness.

If different types of processing unit, considered as different targets, are connected, there arises the problem of compatibility of the different representations of objects passed in rendezvous or messages. There need to be standards for such representations and for the communications protocols to cover the inter-target communication network. It is suggested that these standards be based on the ISO 7-layer reference model [ISO 1982], but oriented specifically to Ada. These standards are not further considered in this guide, whose scope is limited to portability of Ada programs between single processor targets.

The above discussion is pertinent to timing considerations. A distributed system is not likely to have a unique CALENDAR. However, if the system can be treated as a single target, which is assumed, then the accuracy of the clock, e.g. DURATION'SMALL, is the same (as is SYSTEM.TICK). The synchronization of the clocks can be left to run-time support, and it is assumed that the implementation can keep clocks adequately synchronized e.g. to within the overhead time of a rendezvous. If the distributed system were, on the other hand, composed of a number of different target machines, such assumptions would be invalid; and standards would be required for timing and synchronization over the network connecting the targets.

9.3 Task Execution - Task Activation

Mandatory: No assumption should be made about the order of activation of task objects declared in the same declarative list. There must not be side-effects in the declarations of such task objects, see 6.5.

Note: The order is deliberately left undefined in the manual.

The time taken to activate a task could lead to unexpected run-time overheads.

9.4 Task Dependence - Termination of Tasks

Note: The language does not define whether tasks declared in a library package are required to terminate. Hence any program using such packages cannot be sure of when it has reached normal termination.

9.5 Entries, Entry calls and Accept Statements

There are two issues concerning ordering which may give rise to portability problems.

Firstly, although calls are processed in order of arrival on a queue, the times taken for the calls to reach the queue may vary, particularly in a distributed system.

Secondly, the order of evaluation of the parameter associations is not defined by the language.

Mandatory: No assumptions should be made concerning the order of processing of calls in a queue with respect to the issuing of those calls.
Entry parameters must not have side effects affecting other parameters of the same entry.

Information from implementors: Whether there are any restrictions on the range of entry families.

Note: see 6.4.1 and 6.5.

9.6 Delay Statements, Duration, and Time

The type DURATION is machine dependent and its use can therefore give rise to problems.

Mandatory: Values of type DURATION must be within the range -86400.0 .. 86400.0.

Information from implementors: Indication of the likely increase in delay beyond that specified in a delay statement e.g. caused by rescheduling.

Aid: Programming aids to provide estimates of execution time would be useful.

Information from implementors: Range and delta of DURATION.

Note: Type DURATION is a fixed point type and hence its portable use is dependent upon the properties of such types, see 3.5.9.

As regards the information from implementors, any program using timing is likely to rely on a certain degree of accuracy. This may be inferred from DURATION'SMALL; but a delay may be more than expected due to scheduling time and/or shortage of processing power.

It should also be observed that a regular loop programmed as in the example in LRM 9.6 is only guaranteed to give the anticipated interval if it is a model number of the type DURATION.

9.7.1 Selective Waits

The order of evaluation of guards is not defined and the selection among open alternatives is arbitrary.

Mandatory: Evaluation of guards must not have side effects changing the state of other guards in the same selective unit.

The program should not rely on the algorithm used to choose between several open alternatives.

Recommended: Guards should only depend upon local variables of the task in order to avoid the possibility of side effects.

Note: See section 6.5.

9.7.2 Conditional Entry Calls

Note: In a distributed system the definition of 'immediately' may not be as expected.

9.7.3 Timed Entry Calls

Note: In a distributed system the definition of 'immediately' may not be as expected.

9.8 Priorities

Mandatory: A program must not rely upon the use of priorities to enforce synchronization.

Recommended: No assumptions about the range of values that can be specified in the PRIORITY pragma should be made. Similarly, no assumption about the number of different priority levels should be made.

Information from implementors: Range of the subtype PRIORITY.

Note: If a task A has a higher priority than task B, then A cannot rely upon task B not executing when task A is executing because there may be several processors.

Since the number of priority levels is implementation defined, it is advisable to isolate the level values by, for example, making them constants in a package:

```
package PRIORITIES is
   HIGH_PRIORITY: constant PRIORITY := ... ;
   LOW_PRIORITY: constant PRIORITY := ... ;
end PRIORITIES;
```

Other parts of the system then need only refer to these constants.

9.9 Task and Entry Attributes

It should be remembered that E'COUNT only gives the momentary value of the number of queued tasks. Tasks may be removed from a queue by abnormal termination and timed calls. Likewise T'CALLABLE and T'TERMINATED only give the momentary value of the task state.

9.9 Task and Entry Attributes

The use of the attribute T'STORAGE_SIZE needs care. It can be used defensively to protect against running out of storage but clearly the storage used for particular constructs cannot always be predicted or determined.

9.10 Abort Statements

Use of the abort statement can affect the portability of programs because the resulting action is unsynchronized.

Mandatory: No assumption should be made about the moment at which the task being aborted becomes terminated.

9.11 Shared Variables

A shared variable is one which is accessed by more then one task (counting the main program as a task).

Mandatory: A program which is to be moved onto a distributed machine must not contain shared variables accessed by tasks in different components of the machine.

Recommended: The pragma SHARED should not be used.

Information from implementors: Whether there are any restrictions on the use of shared variables.

Note: Although the use of shared variables is generally bad practice there are some circumstances where the unsynchronized use of shared variables may be appropriate. A typical example might be in a process control system where input measurements are gathered by one task and placed in a shared data area from where they may be read as required by other tasks; in many cases it does not matter that other tasks use values that are not all from the same generation.

The objects to which the pragma SHARED can be applied are implementation defined.

10

Program structure and compilation issues

A program is a collection of one or more compilation units submitted to the compiler in one or more compilations. This definition does not guarantee that such a collection, once translated, can be executed - each compilation unit merely specifies the separate compilation of a construct.

A construct may be a subprogram declaration or body, a package declaration or body, a generic declaration or body or a generic instantiation. Furthermore, it may be the body of a subprogram, package, task unit or generic unit declared within another compilation unit: in this case the construct is a subunit.

10.1 Compilation Units - Library Units

A subprogram that is a library unit can be used as a main program. Each main program acts as if called by some environment task. The means by which this execution is initiated are not prescribed by the language definition.

An implementation may impose certain requirements on the parameters and on the result, if any, of the main program. However, every implementation is required to allow, at least, main programs that are parameterless procedures.

Mandatory: The main program must be a parameterless procedure.

Information from implementors: The means of initiation of a main program.

10.3 Order of Compilation

A compilation unit is potentially affected by a change in any unit it depends on. If a compilation unit is successfully recompiled, the compilation units potentially affected by the change are obsolete and must be recompiled unless they are no longer needed. An implementation may be able to reduce the compilation costs if it can deduce that some of the potentially affected units are not actually affected by the change.

The subunits of a unit can be recompiled without affecting the unit itself. Similarly, changes in a subprogram or package body do not affect other compilation units (apart from the subunits of the body) since these compilation units only have access to the subprogram or package specification. An implementation is only allowed to deviate from this rule for inline inclusions, for certain compiler optimizations, and for certain implementations of generic units.

If a pragma INLINE is applied to a subprogram declaration given in a package specification, inline inclusion will only be achieved if the package body is compiled before units calling the subprogram. If a calling unit is compiled before the package body, the pragma may be ignored by the compiler for such calls.

Information from implementors: Whether the implementation checks that units potentially affected by a change are not actually affected.

What additional dependencies between compilation units the implementation creates.

Whether pragma INLINE is ignored for calls of a subprogram compiled before compilation of the subprogram body, and, if so, whether a warning is issued that inline inclusion was not achieved.

10.4 The Program Library

Information from implementors: The form of commands for creating a program library, the form of commands for acquiring and reusing units of other program libraries

10.4 The Program Library

in the same programming environment, the mechanism by which compilation units become the property of a program library, the form of commands for interrogating a program library to discover its contents and the status of those contents; the effect of a compilation failure on program libraries.

10.5 Elaboration of Library Units

The elaboration of library units and their corresponding library unit bodies is performed in an order consistent with the partial ordering defined by the with clauses. An order of elaboration that is consistent with this partial ordering does not always ensure that each library unit body is elaborated before any other compilation unit whose elaboration necessitates that the library unit body be already elaborated. If the prior elaboration of library unit bodies is needed, this can be requested by a pragma ELABORATE. The elaboration of the compilation units of the program is performed in some order that is otherwise not defined by the language.

Compilers are not required to provide either compilation-time or run-time detection of incorrect order dependencies. If a compiler is able to recognize at compilation time that the elaboration of the compilation units in a different order would have a different effect then the compiler is allowed to generate code that raises the exception PROGRAM_ERROR. Alternatively, compilers are allowed to generate code that checks at run-time for this, and to raise PROGRAM_ERROR if the check fails.

Every library unit mentioned in a pragma ELABORATE must have a library unit body.

Recommended: A compilation unit should specify a pragma ELABORATE for every library unit mentioned in the unit's with clauses.

Every library unit which is a package should have a library unit body, even if it is of the form:

```
package body P is
end P;
```

Note: As an example of the problem of the undefined order of compilation unit elaboration, consider the following:

```
package A is
   I: INTEGER := 10;
end A;

with A; use A;
package B is
   J: INTEGER := I;
end B;

package body A is
begin
   I := 20;
end A;
```

The declaration of B and the body of A may be elaborated in either order. If the declaration of B is elaborated first, then J will have the value 10; if the body of A is elaborated first, then J will have the value 20. Consequently, there is an "incorrect order dependence" here (LRM 1.6(d)), which, if the compiler can detect it, may result in the raising of PROGRAM_ERROR. Thus, depending on the implementation, three outcomes are possible:

(a) J = 10,

(b) J = 20,

(c) The exception PROGRAM_ERROR is raised.

The only facility the language provides to overcome this (and to ensure consistent behaviour) is to use the pragma ELABORATE in package B to ensure that the body of A is elaborated first. (Note that in this example, the reference to I in B could be due to a typing error when 1 was required; longer identifiers and fully qualified names are recommended.)

10.5 Elaboration of Library Units

10.6 Program Optimization

Optimization of the elaboration of declarations and the execution of statements may be performed by compilers.

Information from implementors: Details of optimizations performed.

Note: Moving to a compiler that does not do certain optimizations may result in time or space requirements not being met by the compiled program.

11
Exceptions

11.1 Exception Declarations

Mandatory: No assumption should be made as to the precise conditions under which CONSTRAINT_ERROR, NUMERIC_ERROR, PROGRAM_ERROR, TASKING_ ERROR or STORAGE_ERROR exceptions are raised.

11.2 Exception Handlers

Recommended: Exception handlers should not be provided for handling the predefined exceptions NUMERIC_ERROR, PROGRAM_ERROR or STORAGE_ERROR explicitly or implicitly via 'others'.

Note: The practice of defensive programming may require provision of handlers for these exceptions. The portability recommendation is intended to emphasize that the precise conditions which cause the exceptions to be raised may vary from one target/implementation to another. In practice a program may handle these exceptions and still achieve adequate levels of portability.

If the program is such that the conditions which would give rise to the exception can be predicted with certainty it is more portable to explicitly program the detection and handling of these exceptional conditions.

11.7 Suppressing Checks

The SUPPRESS pragma is a recommendation to the compiler that certain run-time checks for exceptional conditions need not be generated. If an error can arise which would then not be dealt with, the program is erroneous. Suppression does not prevent the exception from being raised. The SUPPRESS pragma may not be acted upon.

Mandatory: The SUPPRESS pragma must not be used to achieve any change in the meaning of a program.

Recommended: A check should not be suppressed unless it can be proved that the corresponding exception cannot occur within the scope of the suppression.

12

Generic units

12.1 Generic Declarations

For the elaboration of the generic part, the order of evaluation of generic formal parameters is defined, so the problem of side-effects is reduced. However expressions may appear in the generic part and the rule about side-effects then applies, see 4.5.

12.3 Generic Instantiation

Generic actual/formal parameter substitution follows the same static binding rules as non-generic actual/formal substitution for subprogram calls, discriminant constraints, etc.

The LRM permits a generic program unit body to be compiled separately from its specification. In the following case, however, use of such a compilation unit structure may introduce a dependency between the units which a compiler is entitled to reject as illegal but which may be allowed by some implementations.

```
generic
package A is
   -- specification
     ...
end;
package body A is separate;
package HORROR is new A;
```

(The body of A requires its ancestor to be in the program library, but the ancestor cannot be compiled without the body for A being already available in compiled form).

In some cases, such as a large package with a generic function parameter, it may be essential for an implementation to share code between generic instantiations.

Mandatory: If code sharing is required for effective

implementation, the program documentation must state this.

Programs must not depend on the order of evaluation of actual generic parameters, see 6.5.

Recommended: An instantiation of a generic unit whose body is compiled separately from its specification should not appear in the same compilation unit as the generic specification.

Information from implementors: Under what circumstances code or read-only data will be shared between different instantiations of the same generic unit, and the control (if any) the user may exercise over this.

Note: An implementation which does not share code may give rise to a considerable space penalty. However, code sharing may in some circumstances give rise to a significant run-time penalty.

12.3 Generic Instantiation

13
Representation clauses and implementation-dependent features

13.1 Representation Clauses

Use of representation clauses and implementation dependent features generally leads to non-portable programs, but it is recognized that in certain circumstances they have to be used. They should be localized, e.g. in a package body with a machine independent package specification.

An implementation may limit representation clauses to those that can be handled simply by the underlying hardware. Although mappings acceptable to an implementation do not, according to the LRM, alter the net effect of a program, this assumes that the program is not time or space critical and that the behaviour of the program does not depend for example on relative execution speed of tasks within it. If representation clauses have to be used, they should generally be encapsulated in packages, see Chapter 7. However, representation clauses for the control of task storage and size of collections of access storage may be used to increase portability.

Recommended: Representation clauses should not be used, except perhaps as explained in 3.5.9 and 4.8.

Information from implementors: The effect of PACK.

Note: The pragma PACK is probably the safest means of controlling mapping as regards portability, but it may be ignored by the compiler.

13.5 Address Clauses

These are the least portable of representation clauses, as the location or address defining integer is so open to interpretation, besides having the usual problems of integers. Therefore encapsulation is especially important.

Any program using an address clause to achieve overlays or to link an interrupt to more than one entry is erroneous.

Mandatory: Address clauses must not be used to attempt to overlay code or data, or to link an interrupt to more than one entry.

Information from implementors: Interpretation of the value given in an address clause which associates an entry with an interrupt.

Note: Interrupts should be used with caution, since they are inherently machine-dependent.

13.7 The Package System

Although the package SYSTEM must be defined for any implementation, and it is assumed that the LRM is referring to the target characteristics rather than host, it should not be used as a general rule. It is possible to achieve portability between particular machines by writing separate machine dependent parts for each and selecting the correct one by interrogating SYSTEM_NAME. However, as yet there is no consistent notation for naming machines, and there is the problem of how to name a machine that is intended to look like another machine. Therefore it is better to interrogate machine characteristics other than SYSTEM_NAME. For example, one might have separate algorithms for different ranges of integers supported by anticipated targets, and then choose an algorithm by interrogation of MIN_INT and MAX_INT. This leads to greater portability than with SYSTEM_NAME, but in general it is not possible to cover all possible targets.

The pragma SYSTEM_NAME, even together with pragmas STORAGE_UNIT and MEMORY_SIZE, may not force a compiler to select a corresponding complete set of machine characteristics, so it must not be used. The pragma STORAGE_UNIT cannot in general force a compiler to use the specified number of bits for a storage unit, so it must not be used. The pragma MEMORY_SIZE might help to establish free space size for dynamic allocation, and hence increase portability in some sense; however more specific methods are desirable, see 4.8 for example. Implementation defined pragmas to influence representations must not be used. (This is covered by the rule in 2.8.)

Mandatory: The constants SYSTEM_NAME, STORAGE_UNIT, MEMORY_SIZE and any corresponding pragmas must not be used.

The package SYSTEM and representation attributes must not be used, except for isolating and guarding machine-dependent parts of a program, and for specifying storage allocation, see 4.8.

Recommended: Interrogation of machine attributes should not be used except where limited portability is intended, or where it can be shown that all possible targets are covered.

Information from implementors: Besides the requirements Appendix F of the LRM, the effect of the pragmas SYSTEM_NAME, STORAGE_UNIT and MEMORY_SIZE.

13.8 Machine Code Insertions

Recommended: Machine code insertion should not be used.

Information from implementors: Conventions for writing machine code inserts.

Note: Sometimes machine code is deemed necessary, where efficiency is particularly important or where the program has to interface with special hardware. In order that portability, reliability and legibility are not compromised, machine code insertion should be localized and clearly identified. Great care must be taken over register and calling conventions for the machine code not to interfere with other code, especially if the compiler is liable to be changed.

13.9 Interface to Other Languages

Recommended : The pragma INTERFACE should not be used.

Information from implementors: Conventions for the use of the pragma INTERFACE.

Note: Similar conditions to those of 13.8 apply.

13.10 Unchecked Programming

Unchecked conversion on one implementation may not be possible on another. Unchecked deallocation (see 4.8) and unchecked conversion may result in erroneous programs.

Mandatory: UNCHECKED_CONVERSION must not be used except for output of diagnostic information.

Note: For UNCHECKED_DEALLOCATION see 4.8.

14
Input-output

Conversion of the representation of data as it passes between machines is outside the scope of this guide. Likewise matters concerning the attachment of peripheral devices (e.g. discs) are outside the scope.

14.1 External Files and File Objects

The main problems with files are their naming, length, storage and the meaning associated with 'external'.

The LRM states that the naming conventions have to be established between users. Some filing systems allow reference to a given file by more than one character string, e.g. dependent on the user's current directory. The LRM does not specifically exclude such aliasing, or even dynamic aliasing. For example, when establishing a new external file a 'full' name might be given, corresponding to the path from the top of a file naming hierarchy. Subsequently abbreviations of this name might be used if unambiguous from the context.

In many applications it is desirable for the programmer to be able to consider files as being of indefinite size. However, certain implementations may have limits on file size - e.g. no larger than disc capacity. This guide does not suggest any guaranteed lower limit.

The amount of storage available for files is target dependent. Creation and/or extension of files suffers the problems of dynamic storage allocation, and of deallocation when or after they are deleted. After deletion and if there are no associated internal files, the external file 'can cease to exist', see LRM 14.1.1. This is exactly analogous to objects created by 'new' :- 'When such an object becomes inaccessible, the storage it occupies can be reclaimed (but need not be), depending on the implementation', LRM 4.8.

SIZE as a function is not to be confused with SIZE as an attribute. The latter applied to a file is ambiguous and should not be used. Incidentally it could be argued that because the attribute is of type INTEGER, a file or object of any type must be storable within INTEGER'LAST bits. This however would be far too restrictive on a file when INTEGER'LAST may be only 2**15 - 1. SIZE seems meaningless when applied to printer output, for example.

Mandatory: Aliasing of file names must not be used.

A program must not rely on files being of unlimited size.

Suggested: The PACK pragma should be applied to record or array types used in files if there is otherwise any danger of the file size exceeding the implementation limit.

The attribute SIZE must not be applied to a file.

Information from implementors: Naming conventions, length restrictions, storage restrictions, storage allocation time, deallocation time, and possible direct and indirect association of peripherals for files.
Effect of plugging and unplugging peripherals.
Storage allocation strategy - paging etc.

Note: There could be run-time surprises in both space and time consumed by an operation. For example a WRITE might 'bust' a page, so there could be a hiccup while a page of free storage is allocated.

14.3 Text Input-Output

File limitations could apply to the text of a program on a host, as well as to text files on the target.

Mandatory: Line and page formatting must be done using

NEW_LINE and NEW_PAGE subprograms, rather than explicitly writing end-of-line or end-of-page characters.

Recommended: A program must not have more than 2**15-1 lines.

No textual file or program should have a line of over 80 characters, see also 2.2 and the note below.

Note: A restriction of 80 character positions per line is assumed on target as well as host output devices. If the line length of a file is unspecified, the NEW_LINE subprogram must be called after every group of 80 other characters or less.

14.6 Low Level Input-Output

This tends to be not only target machine dependent but also device dependent.

Mandatory: Package LOW_LEVEL_IO must not be used.

Annexes

Most of the portability aspects of Ada are covered in the main part of the guide. However use of the pragma OPTIMIZE could affect portability and is not mentioned elsewhere.

Mandatory: A program should not rely on action taken on the OPTIMIZE pragma.

STYLE GUIDE

1
Introduction

1.1 Portability and style

The subject of programming style frequently arose during meetings of the Ada-Europe Portability Working Group when discussing portability of programs. Style affects portability; this applies to both the portability of programs from one machine to another (see Portability Guide 1.2) and the portability of programmers from one project to another. It was thus natural for the working group to consider style guidelines after producing portability guidelines.

1.2 Definition of style

Style is the manner of writing as opposed to the matter to be expressed. This guide is not particularly concerned with standards for spelling, capitalization, punctuation, and typographical arrangement, as much of this is covered by the LRM (Ada Language Reference Manual [ANSI 1983]). Style here has nothing to do with the syntax and semantics of the Ada language, which are well defined. Rather the guide is concerned with how Ada should be used to contribute towards legibility, maintainability, correctness, etc. of the program (see objectives below).

1.3 Related work

Here should be mentioned the Style Guide [Abbott 1982], and its shorter counterpart [Abbott & Booch 1982], which were reviewed by the working group who felt that they were somewhat complementary to the group's guide, as they address an earlier stage in program design without being particularly specific to the Ada language. The short Intellimac guide [Gardner *et al.* 1983] was obtained too late for consideration.

The language-independent rules of software engineering,

already well established in recent work in the field of programming, apply in the main to Ada as much as to other languages. Indeed many of the constructs in Ada give language support to the programming design methods evolved elsewhere (see the Yourdon method [Page-Jones 1980], the Jackson method [Jackson 1975,1982], the Mascot method [Mascot 1980] and methods proposed by Dijkstra [Dijkstra 1976] and Dahl [Dahl et al. 1972]). Concepts of modularity, hierarchy, cohesion and coupling will be recognized by readers as motivating many of the rules given in this guide. Style should also include concerns for ease of correct reasoning (informal proof) about programs. Anna can be considered in this connection [Krieg-Brueckner et al. 1982]. In practice the style to support informal proofs also supports the use of formal proofs [McGettrick 1982].

This guide addresses style for programming-in-the-large as well as programming-in-the-small, concepts from [DeRemer & Kron 1976]. The sight of the wood must not be lost for seeing trees. Ada provides mechanisms and facilities to allow assembly of a program from independently produced software components. The meaning of 'program' in this guide should be taken in that context.

After this guide there is a section which includes a bibliography of papers and books relevant to stylistic issues. Some of these are referred to in the comment following a rule.

1.4 Objectives

This guide has been written with a view to helping not only programmers but also those who need to examine programs post facto, e.g. for quality assurance. The rules have been formulated with this in mind.

For programmers this guide is intended to help those who have learned Ada and want to improve their use of the language. It may help those who are accustomed to programming in some other language and find themselves adopting a style more appropriate to that language than to Ada. It may also help those who are familiar with Ada to improve their style.

One of the main aims of adopting a good programming style must be to communicate meaning to people. In the simplest situation, the meaning of the program may only need to be communicated back to the original programmer. However in most projects there will be a team in which more than one person will have an interest in any one program. There may be several writing it, someone to manage progress, someone to check it visually, someone to test it running, someone to integrate it with other programs into a system, and, later on, someone to maintain it. Ada programming style must help anyone who needs to read the source text.

The above considerations of style essentially concern legibility. Another aim for style must be to reduce programming errors in the original source text, mainly by increasing logical clarity. The cost of correcting mistakes increases as the time between their origination and discovery increases, and it must generally be cheapest to avoid mistakes in the first place.

Program reliability improves with legibility and logical clarity, but may also be improved by "defensive programming", i.e. guarding against errors (see 1.7j below).

Another aim of adopting a good style may be to improve program portability. Sometimes the necessary portability can be achieved simply by following the rules of the portability guide, but there are inevitably situations where a program has to be modified to allow it to run on a different machine. A good style should ease such modification. Indeed many of the considerations of the portability subgroup in producing the portability guide were deferred to this guide.

Note that the rules of this guide are not intended to apply to automatically generated text, which therefore should not be unjustifiably criticized for nonconformance, assuming that such automatically generated text is maintained by regeneration.

1.5 Design methods

Design methods can help the programmer to write a program from scratch, whereas style is really a matter of how the program looks when complete. However design and style cannot be divorced, and good design should lead to good style. It is recommended that a design method is adopted which leads to well structured programs.

1.6 Form of the guide

Some general rules for style are given in subsection 1.7 below. The remaining rules are given in chapters 2 to 14, and are listed in subsections whose numbering corresponds to the LRM, such that each rule is listed against the Ada feature to which it applies, as far as possible.

Explanations, comments and examples follow the rule to which they apply. Rules are not presented necessarily in the order that they should be applied or in order of importance. Indeed, some rules may conflict with others in certain situations, and in these situations it is a matter of judgement which rules to apply.

1.7 General rules

All these rules have a bearing on the overall program structure.

a) The program should reflect its role as a model of the problem to be solved, by structure and choice of identifiers.

The reader is more likely to be familiar with the problem or application area (i.e. problem domain) than with the solution! Any uncertainty about what the problem is should be noted, for example if the specification is ambiguous, or appears incorrect. Of course such uncertainty should be resolved if possible.

It is generally useful to the reader to have a glossary of terms. The IEEE has produced a "standard" glossary [IEEE 1982]. If an existing glossary is not used, a glossary could be added to the program to define terms used within it.

b) The approach to the solution of the problem should be clear.

A reader will form a hypothesis about the approach even before starting to read the program, and, as he or she starts to read, this hypothesis will either be supported or contradicted. It is therefore important to lead the reader gently in the right initial direction, for example by means of suitable comment at the beginning of program units. Associated documents and background reading could also be mentioned.

c) The program should be consistent.

Terminology, use of identifiers, layout and style generally must be consistent within the program otherwise the reader is liable to be confused, and it will be difficult to check the program. (But a program that uses independently written packages cannot necessarily conform to their standards.) Conventions should not be flouted without good justification.

d) Unnecessary complication should be avoided.

Elegant simplicity is the hallmark of good design. The program should not be an exhibition for programmer cleverness, even for efficiency - as at a later date it may not be possible to change the program in order to improve it!

As far as possible the program should be succinct, avoiding unnecessary or unhelpful redundancy (e.g. repetition), but the program should not be cryptic. In particular the same function (in the general sense) should not be repeated in two different places [Page-Jones 1980].

e) The program should use existing packages and techniques where appropriate.

Wheels should not be reinvented. The program design should be based on a proven technique if possible. Any existing application packages should be used, when appropriate. Analogies may be taken from other fields, but with care not to confuse the reader.

When a new package is needed, it should be made of sufficient generality to cover possible uses (see 7h). The new package can be regarded as a potential product.

f) Appropriate data abstraction should be employed.

Concepts from the problem area should lead naturally to the definition of data types and operations. The nature of information passed between subsystems or held by subsystems should be suggested by the choice and names of data types, passed as parameters or used within the subsystems respectively. Programmer-defined types can be regarded as extensions to the language, to tailor it to the application.

States of physical objects are naturally modelled by data values. Their behaviour is modelled by providing subprograms which operate on these data to produce sequences of values corresponding to the required sequences of states. The data and operations on it may be encapsulated in a package or packages, such that the only means of accessing the data is through one of the appropriate subprograms.

Advantage should be taken of Ada's strong typing wherever possible. Enumeration types should be used where the choice of enumeration literal can be meaningful. Types should also be used to ensure compile-time consistency checking, for example by defining SPEED, RANGE, etc. rather than using INTEGER say. (However for new types the resulting benefit in checking must be weighed against any added complexity in introducing operations on these types, even though no run-time overheads might be involved.)

g) Unnecessary visibility should be avoided; detail of the implementation of a program unit should be hidden from the user.

Ada allows the implementation to be hidden in the body, with only the relevant aspect of the program unit visible to the user (e.g. caller) of the unit. The principle of information hiding as proposed by Parnas [Parnas 1972b] should be applied, see Chapter 7. The program unit considered as a model should hide the way that the intended behaviour is obtained (as opposed to what that behaviour is) from the rest of the program. Thus "unnecessary" detail should be hidden.

It is, of course, possible to go too far with this rule and produce excessive fragmentation of the program, for example by introducing blocks just to reduce the scope of variables slightly.

h) Related data or code should be grouped, and unrelated data or code should not.

This applies at all levels. The reader expects objects which are grouped together to be related and will form or modify his 'hypothesis' (see b above) accordingly. Packages are particularly useful for grouping things. At a lower level, composite types should be used to obtain data structuring, with related items held in arrays or records, rather than as individual objects.

i) Independency should be exploited.

The program should be modularized in such a fashion as to leave simple interfaces between the parts. Side effects and sharing of data should be avoided, but where sharing of data or code is naturally required, e.g. for data abstraction, the shared part should be encapsulated.

The program should also be modularized so that each part can be easily tested, and tested independently of the other parts (see [Mascot 1980] and [Adrion _et al_. 1982]).

In general, code implementing high level control (decision making) should be separated from code implementing the actions selected (see [Page-Jones 1980] page 137).

j) The program should guard against errors but not be overdefensive.

The degree of defence required will generally depend on the application. However sometimes defence is possible at no significant extra programming cost, and is then always advisable.

There are three kinds of error to defend against:

(i) The error from outside the program. Thus, for example, one should generally have range constraints on parameters passed to the program, checks on input data, etc.

(ii) The simple internal error. This can often be guarded against by taking advantage of strong typing, range constraints on integers, etc. (see 1.7f). In general the program should be written in such a way that as many errors as possible are detected at compile time.

(iii) The error in one part of a program arising from the way another part has been written. For an example of this (see 6c, 11c and [Curry 1982]). Parts of the program used by other parts should be written in such a way as to minimize the chance of misuse.

One of the main aims of defensive programming is to make the program more maintainable, i.e. more easily changed without unforeseen repercussions. A change in part A of a program may affect part B. Ideally the parts should be written either so that B is unaffected by the change in A or so that the compiler will detect if B is not changed to match the change in A. The danger is that B continues to be compiled and executed as if correct, though now incorrect.

k) Asymmetrical relationships should be exploited to produce a hierarchical structure.

In general program units should form a tree structure, with high level units using or calling the lower level units. It is also advisable to separate functionally independent levels amongst the units, such that a unit at one level can only use or call a unit at the next level down. It is particularly dangerous to have two tasks calling one another. However if units are strictly symmetrical in their relationship, they must be at the same level.

Library packages may be shared by all elements of a tree. When a unit is shared one no longer has a tree structure, but one can still retain a layered structure. In general each level should deal with its own resources, acquiring and returning them appropriately (see 11.2c).

l) Program units should not be too large.

The modularity offered by Ada should be exploited, by use of packages for example. This helps to limit the scope of identifiers (see rule m below and 8a). Care must be taken in the layout of program text on pages of listing so that the reader does not have to do an excessive amount of cross-referencing and page turning. A useful concept is that of the "headful". The amount of information that a program reader needs to comprehend at any one time should be limited to such a headful.

However, modularization can be taken too far, and the program must not be too fragmented.

m) The scope of identifiers should be limited.

This rule has similar reasons to those of the previous rule, but note the following rule.

n) Excessive nesting should be avoided.

Excessive nesting reduces the legibility of the program, and can easily be avoided [Clarke _et al_. 1980].

o) Static forms are preferable to dynamic forms.

For example, static expressions, evaluated at compile time, are preferable to dynamic expressions, evaluated during execution of the program. With static forms, the reader can more easily satisfy himself of the correctness of an algorithm. Of course, if the application demands dynamic values, they must be used. (Beware of programs converted from Pascal which may use static forms by mistake.)

p) Indeterminacy should only be used where needed.

Ada allows a degree of indeterminacy, but its use should be limited and confined. Tasks should only be used when their concurrency is really needed.

q) Each feature of the Ada language should be used as and when appropriate, and not in excess.

This is an obvious general rule, and the remainder of this guide is really concerned with the "decomposition" of this rule into separate rules against each feature. In a language such as Ada, a functionally "correct" program can be achieved in many different ways. At one extreme, it may really be a program naively translated from another language and dressed up as Ada; at the other extreme, it may use complex features totally unnecessarily. In either case, the cost in development and maintenance is likely to be higher than if a good style were used.

To summarize, the following general rules apply:-

a) The program should reflect its role as a model of the problem to be solved, by structure and choice of identifiers.
b) The approach to the solution of the problem should be clear.
c) The program should be consistent.
d) Unnecessary complication should be avoided.
e) The program should use existing packages and techniques where appropriate.
f) Appropriate data abstraction should be employed.
g) Unnecessary visibility should be avoided; detail of the implementation of a program unit should be hidden from the user.
h) Related data or code should be grouped, and unrelated data or code should not.
i) Independency should be exploited.
j) The program should guard against errors but not be overdefensive.
k) Asymmetrical relationships should be exploited to produce a hierarchical structure.
l) Program units should not be too large.
m) The scope of identifiers should be limited.
n) Excessive nesting should be avoided.
o) Static forms are preferable to dynamic forms.
p) Indeterminacy should only be used where needed.
q) Each feature of the Ada language should be used as and when appropriate, and not in excess.

2 Lexical elements

"Readability of programs is important, more important than minor implementation details or slight losses in compiler efficiency, and certainly worth thinking about rather than mindlessly copying traditions from the past" [Sale 1979b]. Readability of source text was a particular concern in the design of Ada. If a program can be easily read, it may more readily be understood. Logic errors then become easier to find, alterations can be made more easily, and so the cost of program maintenance is reduced. The textual format of the program should convey its logical structure, and it is recommended that paragraphing should conform to the Ada syntax. Clear indentation and sensible division into pages are essential to the legibility of a program.

This guide does not address the issue of a publication standard for Ada, as proposed for Pascal (see [Bishop 1979] and [Sale 1979a]).

2.1 Character Set

a) Full use should be made of the ISO character set where available.

This gives rise to the following rule.

b) Reserved words should be wholly represented in either lower or upper case characters, and identifiers partly or wholly represented in the opposite case.

The choice of case is highly debatable, and that chosen for the LRM not necessarily the best. The use of lower case for the reserved words is often prefered, so that they do not stand out too much. However lower case is generally easier to read; words can be distinguished by their overall shape, and can be more quickly found when scanning the text. A compromise solution is to use lower case for reserved words and a mixture of lower and upper for other words, starting each part of an identifier with an upper case character and then continuing with lower case until the underscore character if any, as for example in Next_Item.

Variety of case can be used to distinguish different classes of identifier. For example, mixed case can be used for object identifiers, as in Next_Item, but pure upper case for types, such as INTEGER.

The most important point is that lower and upper case should be used consistently. Special care should be taken over the case for delta, digits and range (since these are both reserved words and attributes).

2.2 Lexical Elements, Separators and Delimiters

a) Liberal and consistent use of spacing, both vertical and horizontal, should be made to enhance the readability of the program.

The degree to which this rule should be applied is largely a matter of taste, especially as regards vertical alignment (tabulation). However it is recommended that:

(i) Not more than one source statement or object declaration should occur on a line. (Note that this does not preclude multiple object declarations.)

(ii) Blank lines should be used for grouping related statements and declarations. Spaces should be used to obtain vertical alignment of ':=', '=>' and ':' where the similarity of statements or declarations can usefully be stressed.

(iii) Label, block and loop identifiers should be made clearly visible, by having them to the left of the main text.

(iv) Corresponding bracketing or comb structure reserved words should be aligned on the page. Statements and declarations on the same level should be equally indented. Indentation should be applied consistently, e.g. always by multiples of 5 spaces. For example

```
SWAP :                                  -- Swap integers U and V.
     declare
          TEMP : INTEGER;
     begin
          TEMP := V;
          V    := U;
          U    := TEMP;
     end SWAP;
```

By aligning the matching reserved words, the inherent structure of a program is more clearly seen. Following the reserved words, the next line should be indented to highlight the units of source text (e.g. subprograms, blocks and compound statements) with which the reserved words are identified. In general the layout of examples given throughout the LRM should be followed as this will encourage consistency.

Note that a case statement alternative or an exception handler may sometimes be put on a single line. This is not recommended when it contains a simple statement. Single line alternatives are avoided for consistency in the following example adapted from LRM 5.4

```
case BIN_NUMBER(COUNT) is
     when 1 =>
          UPDATE_BIN(1);
     when 2 =>
          UPDATE_BIN(2);
     when 3!4 =>
          EMPTY_BIN(1);
          EMPTY_BIN(2);
     when others =>
          raise ERROR;
end case;
```

(v) Spaces should be used to obtain vertical alignment of ':=', '=>' and ':' where the similarity of statements or declarations can be usefully stressed.

(vi) Spaces should be used to a certain extent, and consistently, to separate lexical elements within a line. Such spacing should be related to operator precedence, where less or no space indicates higher precedence. For example

```
A := -B * C**2 + F(D, E);
```

(vii) Long lines should be split sensibly. It is better to split a long line than to have it squeezed onto a single line by contravening conventions established for indentation and spacing. The line should be broken in a place that is not likely to mislead the reader as to the semantics of the statement, so for example

```
ALBERT := -BENJAMIN * CHRISTOPHER**2 +
                     FREDERICK(DENNIS, EDMUND);
```

is better than

```
ALBERT := -BENJAMIN
                     * CHRISTOPHER**2 + FREDERICK(DENNIS, EDMUND);
```

or

```
ALBERT := -BENJAMIN * CHRISTOPHER**2 + FREDERICK
                     (DENNIS, EDMUND);
```

2.3 Identifiers

a) Language words with predefined meaning should not be defined or redefined as identifiers without good reason.

Reserved words cannot be redefined by the rules of the language (see LRM 2.9). Other language words comprise the predefined language attributes, pragmas and identifiers of LRM annexes A, B, and C respectively. Predefined identifiers are contained in the package STANDARD, however the names of (and identifiers defined within) the language defined library units listed at the end of annex C should not also be redefined. However the redefinition of identifiers defined within the package ASCII is of no particular concern, as they would normally be prefixed. All language words appear in the LRM index except the identifiers from package ASCII, some from package CALENDAR and some reserved words.

b) Meaningful or simple mnemonic identifiers should be used.

An identifier does not need to be exhaustive in its description of the entity it names (as this would make the program text diffuse and thus difficult to read), but it needs to be sufficiently meaningful for the entity to be recalled without difficulty. Simple mnemonic identifiers are acceptable, but the derivation of the mnemonic must form part of the commentary of the entity declaration. Likewise abbreviations are acceptable, especially if taken from the problem domain, but what they stand for should go in the commentary. Neither mnemonics nor abbreviations should be used for identifiers that occur very few times in the program text (or accompanying documentation).

c) An identifier should not look so similar to anything else that confusion is likely.

Identifiers composed of the upper case letters O and I and lower case l should be avoided, except where a strong convention for their use exists. Identifiers should not differ from one another simply by interchange of letters O, I and l with digits 0 and 1 (and to a lesser importance S with 5 and Z with 2).

d) Identifiers should not differ only by the presence/absence of underline characters.

2.4 Numeric Literals

a) Based numbers should only be used when appropriate to the problem.

Thus, for example, '7**3 + 1' is generally preferable to '7#1001#'.

The use of based numbers will often be machine specific, so should be isolated and encapsulated within the program, thus aiding portability. Their purpose should be commented.

b) Underline characters should be used in long numeric literals.

Decimal digits should be grouped in threes before the decimal point (or from the least significant end if no decimal point). There is a convention to group them in fives after the decimal point. Hexadecimal and binary digits are often best grouped in fours.

c) Upper case 'E' or lower case 'e' should be consistently used for an exponent.

2.4.2 Based Literals

a) Letters in a based literal should consistently be in upper or lower case.

2.6 String Literals

a) Long strings should be broken up at natural boundaries, appropriate to the meaning of the contents of the string if any.

For example

```
"This is an example from the book entitled "
     & "Portability and Style in Ada"
```

Note that a maximum of 80 characters should be assumed for portability (see the portability guide).

There is a problem of representing a number of consecutive spaces so that the number is easy to see. One solution is to have a comment line below the string with dots in positions below the spaces, for example

```
     "  These   words   are   spaced   out  "
--    ..     ...     ...   ...      ...   ..
```

2.7 Comments

a) Comments should be correct, and maintained to remain correct.

A misleading or wrong comment is worse than no comment at all. The comments should be checked for accuracy as much as the rest of the source text, especially after changes to the latter.

b) Comments should be used when they add information for the reader that would not be so immediately visible elsewhere.

The natural places for comments include:

(i) at the head of a program unit, explaining the purpose of the unit, its behaviour in terms of inputs and outputs, any side effects it may produce, exceptions it may pass on, etc. Any dependencies it may have on other parts of the system should also be documented here.

(ii) after declarations (see 3.1a).

Comments should be either boxed to the right of the source text to which they refer or put above in whole lines. In either case the '--'s should be vertically aligned.

c) Comments should abstract above the implementation level as far as possible.

For example

```
J := J + 1;                -- Set index to next element.
```

is obviously better (assuming the comment is correct) than

```
J := J + 1;                -- Add one to J.
```

Indeed, superfluous comments should be avoided.

d) Comments should not confuse specification with implementation.

Comments in a specification part should complete the specification of a program unit, making it sufficient for the user of the unit to obtain all the necessary information without looking at the implementation. These comments should be separated from comments associated with the body, in case the body needs to be subsequently changed.

e) Comments should conform to the usual conventions of prose.

See [Sale 1979b]. However special use of comments to provide formal semantics is an exception, for example see [Gordon 1982]. Quotation of Ada text within a comment should be distinct and be treated consistently, e.g. by enclosure in double quotes.

2.8 Pragmas

a) Pragmas should be made conspicuous by their position in the source text.

Pragmas should generally be placed at the beginning of declarations, etc. A comment should describe the intended effect where not immediately obvious.

3
Declarations and types

3.1 Declarations

a) There should be a comment against each declaration (or group of declarations) to indicate the nature and purpose of what has been declared.

Declarations introduce named entities: they should be commented in an appropriate manner and in sufficient detail to reveal the programmer's understanding of the entity and the purpose for which it was declared. The commentary should make reference to the appropriate part of the deliverable documentation. Of course, if the name of the object is a sufficient description, then no further comment need be given.

However, those properties of an object that it obtains from its type should generally be described in comment against the type declaration rather than the object declaration.

b) Within a large list of declarations of the same general nature, alphabetical ordering should be considered, unless there is a more obvious ordering.

3.2 Objects and Named Numbers

a) Where appropriate, a named number is preferable to a numeric literal.

Use of named numbers greatly improves readability. A named number is preferable to a numeric literal repeated in many statements with the same meaning. However, in some circumstances, a literal is more natural and should be used. For example, in

```
PI : constant := 3.14159;
...
AREA := PI * RADIUS**2;
```

a named number is used for 3.14159, but not for 2. See also 3.2d below.

b) An object should be declared constant if its value is intended not to change.

Use of a constant object improves the reliability of a program since any inadvertent attempt to change its value is detected.

c) A constant object should be used to avoid repetition of a complex expression with constant value.

Readability of a program is improved if a constant object is given the value (and thus replaces) the complex expression. A constant object may be used whenever some expression has a fixed value throughout a code unit (block, subprogram body, etc.) However, a constant object should only be used for an expression that has a meaning in the underlying concept being modelled, not just for an arbitrary expression that happens to remain fixed but has no logical significance. Note that it may be desirable to use a constant object in place of repeated expression evaluation for reasons of efficiency. For example,

```
procedure PROCESS_CIRCLE(C : in CIRCLE) is
     AREA : constant SQUARE_UNITS := PI * C.RADIUS**2;
begin
     if AREA > LOWER_LIMIT and AREA < UPPER_LIMIT then
     ...
```

is good use of a constant object, but

```
procedure PROCESS_CIRCLE(C : in CIRCLE) is
     R_SQUARED : constant SQUARE_UNITS := C.RADIUS**2;
begin
     if PI * R_SQUARED > LOWER_LIMIT and
        PI * R_SQUARED < UPPER_LIMIT then
     ...
```

is not, since the area of the circle has an intrinsic meaning, but the square of its radius has not.

d) A constant object should normally be used rather than a named number.

Named numbers should only be used for values that are truly "universal" and "typeless" (e.g. pi). Usually numbers are not of this kind since they represent particular values of a definite type (see 3.5.4 and 3.5.7). For example,

```
WORD_LIMIT : constant WORD_COUNT := 100;
BIT_LIMIT  : constant BIT_COUNT  := WORD_LIMIT * WORD_SIZE;
```

is better than

```
WORD_LIMIT : constant := 100;
BIT_LIMIT  : constant := WORD_LIMIT * WORD_SIZE;
```

since the two values are not abstract but associated with two distinct entities. If named numbers are used, reliability is prejudiced since the compiler cannot fail code such as

```
if NO_OF_WORDS = BIT_LIMIT then
...
```

even if NO_OF_WORDS is of type WORD_COUNT.

Note that the advantage of a constant object over a named number is lost if it is declared in terms of a predefined type (see 3.2.1c). For example

```
WORD_LIMIT : constant INTEGER := 100;
```

is actually worse than

```
WORD_LIMIT : constant := 100;
```

3.2.1 Object Declarations

a) Associated comments should indicate what the objects represent and how they are expected to be used.

Properties relevant to the objects' type should be commented against the type rather than in the object declarations (see 3.1a).

b) Objects should be initialized.

Programs whose result depends upon an undefined value are erroneous. Thus objects should be given an initial value unless it can be proved that the object is not used before it has received a value. Note that any alteration to the program will require either such proofs to be shown to be still valid or for the program to be resubmitted for proof.

Note that initialization can be by default (see 3.7b, 7(iv) and 7(vi)).

3.3 Types and Subtypes

There are various means of typing in Ada. It is important that the most appropriate is used. Typing is a means of classification of objects, and can be a great help in making a program understandable. Once the reader has understood the meaning and purpose of one object in a class, the classification helps to associate similar meanings and purposes with other objects of the same class.

Typing is associated with data abstraction, and with the association of operations with objects as well as the association of sets of values which the objects can take. Thus typing should be used to associate objects that share operations as well as sets of values.

Typing is also an important means of defensive programming (see 1.7j). Inappropriate operations and values out of range will be automatically detected. The closeness of association of objects can be controlled, e.g. so that they can be used within the same statement with or without type conversion.

a) Separate types should be used for values that belong to logically independent sets, and for distinct concepts.

For example, different types should be used for different dimensions such as mass, length and speed.

If two concepts lead to objects of differing structure (e.g. an array of integers and a single real number), then the need for separate types is clear. However, even if the same structure is involved but the two concepts are distinct, separate types should be used. For example,

```
type X_COORDINATE is digits 6 range 0.0 .. 1.0;
type Y_COORDINATE is digits 6 range 0.0 .. 1.0;
```

b) Subtypes should be used where the addition of range constraints allows concepts to be modelled more closely.

Range constraints are discussed below. Subtypes should be used when the objects involved are truly of the logical kind indicated by the base type and only differ from objects of that type to the extent that the range of values that may occur is restricted. In all other respects, the logical properties of the type and subtype should be the same.

c) Type and subtype declarations should have associated comments to indicate the nature and properties of the classes of object being modelled.

See 3.1a. In particular the comments should record any assumptions the programmer may have made about the nature or properties of the objects.

3.4 Derived Types

a) Derived types should be used for structurally equivalent and related objects.

If two concepts are modelled by the same structure and are also related, derived types should be used, rather than separate types. For example, both a light and a television switch are switches that can be toggled on or off, so we can write:

```
type SWITCH is (ON, OFF);

procedure TOGGLE_SWITCH(A_SWITCH : in out SWITCH) is
begin
    if A_SWITCH = ON then
        A_SWITCH := OFF;
    else
        A_SWITCH := ON;
    end if;
end TOGGLE_SWITCH:
```

```
type LIGHT_SWITCH is new SWITCH;
type TV_SWITCH is new SWITCH;

ANY_SWITCH       : SWITCH       := OFF;
THE_LIGHT_SWITCH : LIGHT_SWITCH := OFF;
THE_TV_SWITCH    : TV_SWITCH    := OFF;
...
TOGGLE_SWITCH(THE_LIGHT_SWITCH);
...
TOGGLE_SWITCH(ANY_SWITCH);
...
THE_TV_SWITCH := TV_SWITCH(ANY_SWITCH);
...
```

The types TV_SWITCH and LIGHT_SWITCH represent similar objects, with similar values and operations, but nevertheless objects of both types are different and so need to be represented by different types. The fact that both are derived from the type SWITCH permits the derivation of operations for this type which are applicable to all the derived SWITCH types. However any operations specified for the type TV_SWITCH are not inherited by the type LIGHT_SWITCH.

Note that a derived type may inherit too much from its parent type, in which case a private type may be more appropriate (see 7.4).

3.5 Scalar Types

a) The ordering of objects of scalar type should not be exploited unless the ordering of the scalar type accurately reflects a logical ordering of the concept to be modelled.

Relational operators and the attributes SUCC and PRED should not be used on values, and FIRST and LAST not used on types, unless the concept is ordered. For example the fact that the position numbers for FALSE and TRUE are zero and one respectively, that BOOLEAN'SUCC(FALSE) = TRUE, and that FALSE < TRUE, should not be exploited.

Note that the ordering of the type CHARACTER may need to be exploited, e.g. for lexographic purposes, and the order usually needed for such purposes is defined in the package ASCII. One should also note that identifiers corresponding to the control characters are not enumeration literals; they are constants of type CHARACTER.

b) Range constraints should be used to allow concepts to be modelled more closely.

The constraints may be exact or may be such that a precise limit cannot be stated, but nevertheless a figure can be quoted that will not be exceeded. For example

```
type HOUR_OF_DAY is range 0 .. 23;          -- exact
type AGE is range 0 .. 150;                -- inexact
```

The exact upper limit for ages is not known, but nobody will be over 150.

However even the full use of such constraints may not solve difficulties of portability (see Portability Guide 3.5).

c) Range constraints should not be relied upon to detect run-time errors due to invalid inputs, etc.

If there is any possibility of invalid run-time data that may have a value outside the range specified for its (sub)type, this should be checked for explicitly. An appropriate exception may then be raised (the cause of which is obvious), rather than CONSTRAINT_ERROR (which may be due to any number of things). This may involve the use of a "temporary" variable, for example;

```
type SENSOR_READING is new INTEGER;
subtype VALID_SENSOR_READING is SENSOR_READING
    range -100 .. 100;
BASIC_READING : SENSOR_READING;
READING : VALID_SENSOR_READING;

BASIC_READING := NEXT_READING (SENSOR);
if BASIC_READING < VALID_SENSOR_READING'FIRST or
   BASIC_READING > VALID_SENSOR_READING'LAST then
    raise SENSOR_ERROR;
end if;
READING := BASIC_READING;
```

All "external" range violations should be handled in this way, ensuring that only valid inputs are processed. Any CONSTRAINT_ERRORs that then arise are due (almost certainly) to some fault in the program.

d) Use of the null range should be clearly indicated by comment.

Use of an upper bound lower than the lower bound to produce a null range is somewhat obscure and needs to be justified in comment.

3.5.1 Enumeration Types

a) An enumeration type should always be used in preference to an integer type unless the logical nature of the concept to be modelled demands the other.

The meaningfulness of identifiers for enumeration literals contributes to the readability of the program.

b) A two-valued enumeration type should always be used in preference to boolean when there exists a suitable word pair for the values.

Our natural handling of antonyms is through word pairs [Atkinson 1979]. By their use, negation and testing for false values can be avoided. There is a mental overhead caused by the inversion of predicates. The enumeration type encourages use of the 'case' statement rather than 'if' statement (see 5.4a).

If the values have some natural ordering, the lesser should be put first in the type definition, e.g. (cold, hot), (low, high), (small, large), (shallow, deep). If not, the values may still differ in positiveness, in which case the less positive should be put first, e.g. (off, on).

3.5.7 Floating Point Types

a) The range and accuracy should be specified to allow concepts to be more closely modelled and for portability.

The reasons are as for 3.5a. Unnecessarily high accuracy should particularly be avoided.

Note that the number of digits in a real number may imply a degree of accuracy to the reader. In floating point expressions, one may want an exact number. This can be converted to a real number in order to satisfy the requirement for a floating point operand. For example, if RADIUS is of floating point type, one can have 'REAL(2) * RADIUS'. Alternatively '*' could be overloaded to allow '2 * RADIUS'. Note that such conversion or overloading is unnecessary for universal expressions, so that one can have '2 * PI * RADIUS' for example (see LRM 4.10). This is an advantage of universal expressions (see 4.4b).

3.5.8 Operations of Floating Point Types

a) Dependence of algorithms upon explicit properties of floating point types should be localized and tightly controlled.

For example, the assumption that FLOAT'DIGITS > 6 can raise portability problems. Large numerical packages should have conventions concerning accuracy, and these conventions must be applied consistently for ease of maintenance. See also 4.1.4.

b) Convergence should be controlled by the use of attributes rather than by the use of explicit constants.

For example, the series A(N) + A(N + 1) + A(N + 2) ..., if convergent and all terms are positive, may be summed by the loop

```
SUM := A(N);
J := N + 1;
while A(J) > SUM * F'EPSILON loop
      SUM := SUM + A(J);
      J := J + 1;
end loop;
```

which automatically terminates when no further accuracy can be obtained.

3.5.9 Fixed Point Types

a) Fixed point types should be defined and used with care.

The only fixed point type that one may be required to use is DURATION (see LRM 9.6). Programming of numerical algorithms is easier with floating point, and the resulting programs easier to maintain. On the other hand, on some machines the performance of floating point may be so poor as to force the use of fixed point. For a further discussion of these issues, see Wichmann [1983].

Integers should be used for values which are inherently exact. For example, integer values of a small currency unit should be used rather than fixed point values of a larger unit.

b) A specific value for SMALL should be set using a representation clause if specific model numbers are required.

3.6 Array Types

a) A record type should be used in preference to an array type, if the components can be sensibly named.

Compare enumeration type versus integer (see 3.5.1a).

An array type should only be used to model a collection of homogeneous objects; if logically different, but connected, objects are involved, a record type should be used. For example, use

```
type TABLE_ENTRY is
     record
          SPEED : SPEED_TYPE;
          RANGE : RANGE_TYPE;
     end record;
TABLE : array(1 .. 50) of TABLE_ENTRY
```

rather than

```
TABLE : array(1 .. 2, 1 .. 50) of INTEGER;
```

where TABLE (1,N) is the speed of Nth entry, and TABLE (2,N) is the range.

b) Special attention should be given to the initialization of array objects.

Array types are especially prone to problems of uninitialized declarations (see 3.2b).

3.7 Record Types

a) Overcomplicated record structure should not be used.

This would reduce readability. Intermediate records may allow structure to be seen more clearly. Related data should be grouped, but unrelated should not (see 1.7h). Excessive nesting should be avoided (see 1.7n).

b) Default initializations should be supplied.

A default initialization ensures that each object has a well-defined value under all circumstances so the program's behaviour will always be predictable and repeatable. If a single default value is not appropriate for all objects, the one that applies for the majority should be used.

Note that the type declaration may be separated from object declarations using that type (e.g. be in a different listing). Under these circumstances, exploitation of the default value may prejudice readability of the program (because it may not be clear what value the object has before an explicit assignment take place). An assignment to set up the object's value may thus be worthwhile, even if strictly redundant.

Default initializations are especially important for private types (see 7.4.1).

3.7.3 Variant Parts

a) Records with variant parts should be used for objects that are basically related and are logically connected, but have some differing parts.

Records with variant parts should not be used for objects that may happen to have some things in common, but are nevertheless not logically connected. For example:

```
type ITEM_OF_FURNITURE(KIND : FURNITURE_KIND := DESK) is
    record
        LENGTH : L_CM;
        HEIGHT : H_CM;
        WIDTH  : W_CM;
        case KIND is
            when CHAIR =>
                WITH_ARMS : YES_OR_NO;
            when CUPBOARD =>
                NO_OF_SHELVES : SHELF_COUNT;
            when DESK ! CABINET =>
                NO_OF_DRAWERS : DRAWER_COUNT;
        end case;
    end record;
```

is a good use of variant parts, since all objects concerned are pieces of furniture. Lots of other, totally unconnected, things have length, height and width (e.g. a room), but the record should not be extended to have a variant part giving the number of windows (for example).

b) Enumeration types should be used for discriminants of record variants whenever possible.

This is in the interests of readability (see 3.5.1a and 3.5.1b). Thus FURNITURE_KIND is an enumeration type in the above example.

c) A default initialization of the discriminant should be given.

If no default value is supplied, each object declaration must include a value for the discriminant, for example:

```
MY_CHAIR : ITEM_OF_FURNITURE(KIND => CHAIR);
```

Such an object would then only be of the kind fixed at declaration time. In contrast, with a default discriminant value, a declaration of the form

```
NEWEST_ITEM : ITEM_OF_FURNITURE;
```

is possible. This variable may then be used for any kind of item (if the complete object is assigned to it).

Note that the benefits of typing may be obtained by subtype declarations such as

```
subtype SEAT is ITEM_OF_FURNITURE(CHAIR);
```

If one wants a "frozen" type, then it should be made a subtype.

3.8 Access Types

a) Access types should only be used when a name is to be associated with different objects at different times.

Classic uses of access types include linked lists, trees and other similar data structures. Such structures use pointers (to successors) that do not have a permanent value. However, access types may be needed for static trees, etc. if this leads to a more consistent programming style throughout the program (such that a static and a dynamic tree are treated identically for example).

b) Excessive indirection should be avoided.

Access types are required for creating lists and trees. However an element in a list or tree should be accessed directly via a single pointer if possible, rather than indirectly via a pointer in a previous element.

Note that an array is preferable to a list as it is more static, see 1.7o, besides allowing more direct access. However, again, consistency may require the use of access types.

c) Details of implementation of a structure with access types should be hidden from the user.

This is a particular case of rule 1.7g. All references to such a structure should be achieved via a procedural or functional interface. Objects of access type should not be passed (as pointers to the structure), except when absolutely necessary for efficiency.

3.9 Declarative Parts

a) A declarative part should start with a description of the overall objective of the declarations it contains and should describe any limitations assumed.

b) A comment should be made if the meaning of the program depends on the order of evaluation of declarations.

Declarations are elaborated in the order in which they appear in the program text. For example, in

```
declare
     J : INTEGER := 0;
begin
     ...
     declare                       -- Order of elaboration
                                   -- of these declarations
                                   -- affects semantics.
          K : INTEGER := J;
          J : INTEGER := 1;
     begin
          ...
     end;
     ...
end;
```

K would be initialized to 1 rather than 0 if declared last.

4

Names and expressions

4.1 Names

a) The name for a type should generally be a common noun indicating the class of the object to which it belongs.

For example:

```
type PET is (CAT, DOG, ...);
type EMPLOYEE is record ...
                 end record;
```

Where appropriate, the type name may be used to indicate the units involved, for example:

```
type ANGLE_DEGREES is ...
type DISTANCE_METRES is ...
```

This subject is discussed in [Abbott 1982].

b) Names of objects should preferably be more precise than names of types.

They may be qualified by a prefix or may be proper names, for example:

```
MY_PET : PET := DOG;
JACK : EMPLOYEE;
```

Note that a task name may be better as a verb rather as a noun, when the task is expressing an action, for example as part of a composite action (see 9e).

c) Enumeration literals should generally be nouns, verbs or adverbs.

Different parts of speech should not be mixed within a type definition. In the case of a two-valued enumeration type, antonyms would normally be used (see 3.5.1b). An adverb might be used as a parameter to a procedure.

d) Names of subprograms and task entries should generally be verbs or nouns.

The name of a procedure or task entry should normally be a verb in the imperative. The name of a function should normally be a noun; but, when returning a boolean value, one should be able to consider it a question (for example 'FREE_LIST_EMPTY' and 'IS_OPEN'), the answer to which is TRUE or FALSE as appropriate.

4.1.2 Slices

a) If a slice is frequently used, the bounds given by the discrete range should be the subject of a subtype declaration.

4.1.4 Attributes

a) Implementation defined attributes should be avoided.

This is mainly for portability, see the Portability Guide 4.1.4.

b) Tests on attributes of the base type and machine or implementation dependent types should be isolated and encapsulated in "lower level" modules.

Tests on attributes should also facilitate "dead code" elimination by the compiler. For example, if one has alternative algorithms depending on the nature of the target, only the selected algorithm need produce object code loaded onto the target.

c) Attributes should be used to provide generality, but should be used with care.

Generally, an attribute should only be used of it is a characteristic on the underlying concept, not merely of the Ada entity used to model the concept. Even in such cases, the use of an attribute should be defensive or to improve clarity. For example given a type

```
type DAY is (MON, TUE, ... SUN);
```

then

```
if TODAY = MON then
    TOMORROW := TUE;
end if;
```

is better than

```
if TODAY = DAY'FIRST then
    TOMORROW := TUE;
end if;
```

However,

```
if TODAY = DAY'LAST then
    TOMORROW := DAY'FIRST;
else
    TOMORROW := DAY'SUCC(TODAY);
end if;
```

is better than

```
if TODAY = SUN then
    TOMORROW := MON;
else
    TOMORROW := DAY'SUCC(TODAY);
end if;
```

because the former remains valid if DAY changes, for example to

```
type DAY is (SUN, MON, ... SAT);
```

The former is, in effect, more general. See also 5.5b.

4.3 Aggregates

a) The 'others' choice should not be used without good reason.

Named or positional aggregates should be used to maintain readability; only when the list of components is prohibitively long or cumbersome should the 'others' construct be used. Use of 'others' may inadvertantly hide an error following a program modification elsewhere. See 5.4b.

4.3.1 Record Aggregates

a) Named aggregates should be used where possible.

The use of a named aggregate enhances readability by making it abundantly clear which values are being assigned to which component of a record.

4.4 Expressions

a) Syntactically redundant parentheses should be used to enhance the readability of expressions by indicating the order of evaluation especially where operator priorities are not as expected in mathematics or where operators are programmer defined.

b) Universal expressions should be used in preference to static (but not universal) expressions, which in turn are preferable to dynamic expressions.

Universal expressions maximize the accuracy/portability; static expressions minimizse the run-time evaluation of expressions. For example

```
KILO : constant := 1_000;
MEGA : constant := KILO * KILO;
...
X := MEGA;
```

is better than

```
KILO : constant INTEGER := 1_000;
MEGA : constant := KILO * KILO;
...
X := MEGA;
```

(because INTEGER'LAST may be less than one million), which in turn is better than

```
KILO : constant := 1_000;
...
MEGA : constant INTEGER := SQUARE(KILO);
...
X := MEGA;
```

c) Unless naturally occurring, negatives, and especially double negatives, should be avoided.

The program should reflect positive thinking [Atkinson 1979]. Rule 3.1.5 is intended with this in mind.

As an example

```
X := A + B - C;
```

is better than

```
X := A - (C - B);
```

unless (C - B) has some significance, such as the difference between the current level and the base level, or because it is used frequently in other different expressions, or because A + B might overflow. Similarly, taking the example of THE_LIGHT_SWITCH from 3.4a,

```
if THE_LIGHT_SWITCH = ON then
```

is better than

```
if THE_LIGHT_SWITCH /= OFF then
```

and 'not FALSE' should never appear in source text.

d) The mixing of 'and's and 'or's in the same expression should generally be avoided.

See [Woodward 1980]. It is easy to be confused by a complex boolean expression, and such expressions can usually be avoided. For example, a complex boolean expression as a condition in an 'if' statement can always be replaced by a number of simpler expressions in a more complex 'if' statement, which may be easier to understand. Mixing of 'and's and 'or's should not be avoided by introducing 'not'; however note that inversion can often be achieved by other means, for example by changing 'A < B' to 'A >= B'. If mixing is necessary, then redundant parentheses should be used to indicate explicitly the order of application of the operators in the evaluation of the expression.

e) Other things being equal, variables should precede constants.

Generally this is the convention, is more natural, and/or follows the pattern of other Ada constructs more closely. For example

```
if A < 10 then
     X := X + 1;
end if;
```

4.5.1 Logical Operators and Short-circuit Control Forms

a) Short-circuit control forms should not be used unless logically necessary.

It may be important that the second operand is not evaluated if the first is FALSE (requiring 'and then') or if the first is TRUE (requiring 'or else'). For example in

```
POINTER /= null and then POINTER.ITEM = 0
```

it is important that the second operand is not evaluated if the first is FALSE.

The short circuit form should not generally be used otherwise. If used to increase efficiency of execution, there should be a comment to this effect. Note that the short circuit form forces a procedural view (rather than a functional/static view) of the expressions in which it occurs, which is somewhat undesirable.

4.6 Type Conversions

a) An explicit type conversion should not be used if a qualified expression can be used instead.

An explicit type conversion should only be used to convert from one type to a different one. Conversion of an object of a particular type to that type may have the same effect as using a qualified expression, but its use is conceptually wrong.

4.7 Qualified Expressions

a) Redundant qualifications may be justified if they make the meaning of the program clearer, but situations where qualification is necessary should be avoided if possible.

Although the context might make qualification strictly redundant (e.g. when other subprogram parameters imply the type of the one in question), the qualification may help the reader understand more easily what is happening.

If possible, duplicated enumeration literals, etc. should be avoided so as to remove the need for qualification, but if the nature of the concept being modelled is such that this cannot be done naturally, it is better to duplicate literals and use qualification. For example, if

```
type FRUIT is (APPLE, ORANGE, PEAR);
```

then using the synonym AMBER in

```
type TRAFFIC_LIGHT is (RED, AMBER, GREEN);
```

is better than duplicating ORANGE, but the most natural form for rainbow colours is

```
type RAINBOW is (RED, ORANGE, YELLOW, GREEN, BLUE,
                 INDIGO, VIOLET);
```

and this should be used even though duplication occurs.

5

Statements

5.1 Simple and Compound Statements - Sequences of Statements

a) Labels should not normally be used.

Labels are used as destinations for goto statements (see 5.9), and are therefore unnecessary.

The use of labels for documenting programs by naming statements is not recommended either, because the reader cannot know whether there is a corresponding goto somewhere else in the program. (This does not include identifiers for blocks and loops, which have different syntax.)

5.2.1 Array Assignments

a) Array slice assignments should be used rather than loops, to copy all or part of an array; they are clearer and less error prone.

For example, to produce a downward shift in the elements of an array A, the assignment:

```
A(1 .. 8) := A(3 .. 10);
```

is equivalent to the loop:

```
for J in 1 .. 8 loop
     A(J) := A(J + 2);
end loop;
```

This loop performs a shift down. If a shift up is required, then the correct assignment:

```
A(3 .. 10) := A(1 .. 8);
```

is not correctly replaced by the loop:

```
for J in 1 .. 8 loop
     A(J+2) := A(J);
end loop;
```

5.3 If Statements

a) If statements should be used for selections of alternatives, when these are selected on the basis of a test (or tests) of boolean conditions.

A binary choice uses:

```
if VALID then
     ...
else
     ...
end if;
```

A choice between many alternatives may be written use the elsif form:

```
if B1 then
     ...
elsif B2 then
     ...
else
     ...
end if;
```

The conditions controlling the choice are not necessarily mutually exclusive.

b) An 'if' statement should not be used to create the effect of a case statement (see 5.4 below) controlled by a value of enumeration type:

The following example shows an if statement which should be replaced by an equivalent case statement:

```
if    TODAY = MON then
      ...
elsif TODAY = TUE then
      ...
end if;
```

5.4 Case Statements

a) Case statements should be used when the selection depends on the value of a single variable or expression of any discrete type except boolean.

In general, enumeration types are preferred to booleans for representing objects with two states (see 3.5.1b). This permits meaningful names to be given to the guards in the case branches.

```
case LIGHT is
     when OFF => ...
     when ON  => ...
end case;
```

A boolean variable is appropriate for logical truth values. A selection controlled by a boolean variable should use an "if" statement. The form

```
case VALID is
     when TRUE => ...
     when FALSE=> ...
end case;
```

should not be used.

b) The 'others' choice should not be used unless there is a good reason; it should not be included as a matter of course.

The use of 'others' reduces the power of the compiler checks and can have consequences for program maintenance. For example consider a situation in which a new value is introduced to an enumeration type, but the appropriate adjustment to a case statement was overlooked. In that case the compiler will not detect the omission if 'others' has been used. Sometimes the use of a subtype for the controlling variable may avoid the need for 'others'.

However, if a dynamic subtype is used for the control, then 'others' is essential.

5.5 Loop Statements.

a) The conditions in which a loop will terminate should be made evident in the program.

If an apparently endless loop is written, the implicit circumstances (exceptions or abortions by other tasks) in which it will terminate must be documented.

b) A 'for' loop should be used to control the repetition in all cases when the number of cycles is determined at the time of loop entry.

Whenever possible the range of the control variable should be given as a complete type or subtype, or as the index range of an array.
For example:

```
for D in DAY loop
     ...
end loop;
for J in A'RANGE loop
     ...
end loop;
```

are preferred to the alternatives

```
        for D in MON .. SUN ...
and     for J in  10 .. 37  ...
```

When the range is given explicitly in terms of the bounds of the index, the programmer must remember details of the type in question, and the program is less robust against changes in the type definition.

Consideration should be given to introducing a subtype when a loop is required over a subrange of some type.

c) If termination depends on a condition which is re-evaluated after each cycle then a while clause should be used.

d) Whenever possible a comment should be included defining the loop invariant.

Assertions which are true throughout the loop body should appear before the loop statement:

```
                                          -- assert {X>0}
while (abs(Y * Y - X) > EPSILON) loop
   ...  -- calculate next iteration for Y
end loop;
```

Assertions which are true after each iteration, but not necessarily so during the steps within the loop, are inductive assertions, and may be used in proving programs correct. These may be placed at the end of the loop body, just before the 'end loop'.

Multiplication by repeated addition preserves the invariant {U * V + R = X * Y} as in the following.

```
R := 0;
U := X;
V := Y;                        -- assert {X > 0}
while U > 0 loop
   U := U - 1;
   R := R + V;
                               -- assert {U * V + R = X * Y}
end loop;
```

This loop terminates with {U = 0 and R = X * Y}.

A further example is given in section 5.7b. For further examples see [McGettrick 1982] and [Kreig-Bruekner _et al_. 1983].

5.6 Block Statements.

a) A block should be used to reduce a compound action to the status of a single statement, if this supports a well-defined abstraction.

Logically unrelated actions should not be grouped in a block (see 1.7d).

Blocks may be thought of as explicitly coded in-line procedures. They should be named for reference and as documentation, and to aid the reader's understanding of the abstraction involved.

b) Declarations of objects used only within the block should be nested within it.

Blocks permit declarations to be localized, reducing the incidence of accidental name clashes, and equally of the obscuring of names from outer units over a greater scope than necessary. A good guide is to consider that no variable should be declared before the data to initialize it is available (see 3.2.1b). However, blocks should not be introduced indiscriminately, and their lengths should be restricted to a reasonable maximum.

c) Declarations in a block should be restricted to variables for temporary working space, constants, renaming declarations and use clauses, and possibly exceptions.

Declarations at block level can include all object classes, variables, types, procedures, functions, etc. However, if a subproblem is sufficiently complex to require an inner procedure, then it should be itself coded as a procedure, rather than a block.

```
EXAMPLE:
     declare
          use COLOUR_IO;
          TEMP : INTEGER := 0;
          X    : constant FLOAT := A(J)**2;
          N    : INTEGER renames CLASS(5).NAME(J).AGE;
     begin
          ...
     end EXAMPLE;
```

d) A block should be used to permit the definition of a local exception handler.

If it is important that an exception should not cause exit from a loop, a block within the loop may contain a handler local to the loop.

The declarative part can be omitted if it is not required. The following example gives the outline of a program which will read an input tape, trying ten times, before finally abandoning the attempt by raising the exception in the outer level.

```
TRIES := 0;
loop
     begin
          TRIES := TRIES + 1;
          READ_TAPE; -- Procedure call to read input tape;
                     -- raises TAPE_ERROR if read fails;
          exit;      -- Success!
     exception
          when TAPE_ERROR =>
               if TRIES > 10 then
                    raise TAPE_ERROR; -- abandon
               else REWIND_TAPE;
               end if;
     end;
end loop;
```

5.7 Exit Statements.

a) Exit statements should be used only when fully justified.

Exit statements break the structure of the loop, and can make the semantics difficult to define. Its use in the example below is considered justified, but the invariant is an incomplete description of the behaviour.

An exit statement may be used when there are several reasons for exit from a loop and these must be distinguished after the termination.

For example, the program to conduct a linear search to find a key KEY in an array A, may be coded:

```
FOUND := FALSE;
for J in A'RANGE loop
     if A(J) = KEY then
          N := J;
          FOUND := TRUE;
          exit;
     end if;
               -- assert {not FOUND and for all K : A'RANGE
               --           (if K <= J then A(K) /= KEY)}
end loop;
```

This separates the concerns of the programmer for what is the range of the index to be scanned, and the possible existence of the KEY in the list.

5.8 Return Statements

a) A return statement should be used to return control to a calling program as soon as the values to be returned have been computed.

Note that this may imply several return statements in different paths of a subprogram. The alternative of storing the returned values for use at a common return point is often clumsy and inefficient.

Note also that there must be at least one return statement in a function.

5.9 Goto Statements

a) Goto statements should not be used.

Use of a goto in other structured languages is often advocated to enable the handling of exceptional conditions and the premature exit from loops. Ada makes provision for these with exceptions and with the exit statement respectively. In a logically constructed program the goto should not be needed.

6

Subprograms

Subprograms provide an important means of structuring a program and implementing a form of operational abstraction. They may also be included in data abstractions (see 1.7f). This structuring can be done in many ways and some rules are needed on how it should be done.

There is no reason to avoid having a subprogram that is used only once. It should be remembered that decomposition into subprograms is a way of structuring the program. The overhead associated with subprogram call and return can sometimes be avoided by specifying the INLINE pragma. This pragma is useful for short subprograms used to provide abstract data types. Note that the pragma is likely to be ineffective if

(i) The subprogram is recursive (self or mutually).

(ii) The subprogram has a separately compiled body.

(iii) The subprogram body contains subunits.

The following rules concern the structuring of a program by including subprograms.

a) A subprogram should have a single logical role in the program and a name of corresponding meaning.

This is the most important rule on the decomposition of a program into subprograms, for comprehension. It promotes the functional cohesion of subprograms [Meyers 1973, 1975]. A procedure name should normally be a verb in the imperative, expressing a simple, specific, direct action that truly reflects the intended role. A function should normally be a noun. See also 4.1.

b) Subprograms should have a suitable length.

The listing of a subprogram should preferably fit in one page. If this is not possible, it may be because the subprogram has not been implemented with a suitable set of supporting subprograms. However such decomposition should not be taken too far. (See 1.7l)

Within a group of closely related subprograms, it may be desirable to have subprograms in alphabetical order when there is no more obvious ordering (see 3.1b).

Nested subprogram, package or task bodies should be 'separate' if they are liable to unduly distance the body of the containing subprogram from its specification (see 10.2a).

c) A subprogram without side-effects returning a single value should be written as a function.

The value should be returned as a function value. The advantage of using a function rather than a procedure is that a function can be called in an expression and supply initialization values for variables which a procedure cannot. However, if there is a side-effect, such as with POP of 7(iii), the program could be erroneous through depending on the order of evaluation of functions in an expression. Having POP as a procedure prevents such misuse (see 1.7j).

d) Recursive subprograms should be used with care.

Recursion is a powerful technique, but one should remember that people may be unfamiliar with it, or even afraid of it. Recursion should be avoided when an iterative solution would be as simple.

6.1 Subprogram declarations

a) A description of a subprogram should be given with its declaration.

With the declaration there should be a description of

(i) the role of the subprogram

(ii) formal parameters

(iii) global variables used (see [Dijkstra 1976])

(iv) side-effects

(v) exceptions to be handled outside the subprogram

(vi) involvement of the subprogram in recursion.

b) Subprograms with equivalent parameters should declare each in the same position and with the same identifier

This rule is meant to make programs more readable by reducing the reader's memory requirement. Parameters that are not equivalent should have different identifiers to avoid confusion.

6.2 Formal parameters

a) Formal parameters should be annotated with their declaration.

They must be fully described, as for other declared objects (see 3.1a).

b) The number of parameters should be kept small.

A large number may indicate that the subprogram doesn't implement a single role, that the functional boundary of the subprogram should be changed, or that the Ada data structuring capabilities have not been utilized (for example, spatial position can be given as one rather than three parameters).

c) The parameter mode indication should be used appropriately in procedures but should not be used in functions.

The mode indication is important information to both compiler and reader. Mode indications 'in', 'in out' or 'out' should be used according to the real usage of the parameter. However for functions all parameters are of mode 'in'; advantage should be taken of the default option to this mode to avoid superfluous text.

d) Parameters should not normally be used as local working space.

Parameters of mode 'in out' and 'out' should normally only be assigned to in order to give their final result in a subprogram. However the space corresponding to 'in out' parameters of array or record type may need to be used for storing temporary values in order to avoid the overheads of copying. Indeed a whole structure should not be passed in order for part of it to be accessed. Passing the whole is called stamp coupling by Yourdon [Page-Jones 1980]. Note that an 'out' formal parameter variable can be assigned but not read.

e) Parameters with default expressions should be used with care.

When a parameter value is not given in a subprogram call the default expression is evaluated and the resulting value is used. Unfortunately neither the fact that there is a defaulted parameter nor its value are conspicuous at the point of the subprogram call. Part of the information is hidden from the program reader. Therefore the mechanism should be used with care. It should only be used where the defaulted parameters have very well known values (i.e. where they are defaulted most of the time and where the default is only over-ridden in special circumstances). An acceptable use of default expressions is given in the LRM 14.3.5 and 14.3.10 to specify the width of formats for input-output.

6.3 Subprogram Bodies

a) Global variables should not be accessed unless necessary.

Access to global variables can lead to aliasing and the kind of error envisaged in 6.2e.

b) Bodies should be textually positioned to avoid unnecessary visibility.

See notes under 1.7g and 8a.

c) The name of the subprogram should be repeated at the end.

6.4 Subprogram calls

a) When a subprogram has terminated by an exception, the 'in out' and 'out' parameters should not be relied upon.

Since the parameter transfer mechanism is unspecified, it is not known if the parameters contain their original values, some intermediate values or the final values after the termination. A program which assumes one of these possibilities is therefore erroneous.

6.7 Overloading of operators

a) Overloading of operators should be used with care.

The operator symbols in programming languages have a very traditional meaning. When new operators are defined they should comply with this meaning. For example, the operator symbol for vector addition should be '+' and no other symbol is really acceptable.

7

Packages

Ada packages should encapsulate sets of related entities, isolating their detailed specifications from the rest of the program. When correctly used, they provide increased security within a program by preventing unauthorized access to information encapsulated within the package. They also contribute substantially to the readability of a large program by limiting the amount of information required to understand a particular part of it.

A package can be used in a number of ways:

(i) Package as a named collection of declarations.

Sometimes there are declarations that belong together and that are used together. They can be put into a package as in this example

```
package WORK_DATA is                    -- specification without body

    type DAY is (MON, TUE, WED, THU, FRI, SAT, SUN);
    type HOURS_SPENT is delta 0.25 range 0.0 .. 24.0;
    type TIMETABLE is array(DAY) of HOURS_SPENT;
    NORMAL_HOURS : constant TIMETABLE :=
        (MON .. THU => 8.25, FRI => 7.0, SAT ! SUN => 0.0);

end WORK_DATA;                          -- end specification
```

Note that this specification has no body.

(ii) Package as a collection of data and operations.

Often one needs to supplement the type and data declarations with operations. The above example could be extended thus

```
package WORK_DATA is

     -- This package implements data structures suitable for
     -- their timetable applications. TOTAL_TIME adds all the
     -- times in the timetable. QUALIFIED_OVERTIME adds all
     -- qualified overtime, i.e. time over nine hours in a
     -- workday plus all time on Saturday and Sunday.

     ...                              -- type and data declarations
     function TOTAL_TIME(T : TIMETABLE)
          return HOURS_SPENT;
     function QUALIFIED_OVERTIME(T : TIMETABLE)
          return HOURS_SPENT;

end WORK_DATA;                        -- end specification

package body WORK_DATA is             -- body

     function TOTAL_TIME(T : TIMETABLE) return HOURS_SPENT is
          ...
     end TOTAL_TIME:

     function QUALIFIED_OVERTIME(T : TIMETABLE)
          return HOURS_SPENT is
          ...
     end QUALIFIED_OVERTIME;

end WORK_DATA;                        -- end body
```

(iii) Package providing protected objects and operations on them.

An important principle to apply, when constructing a program, is that of "information hiding", first discussed in [Parnas 1972a,b]. Packages can be used to hide information from the rest of the program while making explicit the interface with other program parts. This has the advantages that implementation details of each package can be changed by altering only its body, and that the rest of the program may be understood without reference to these details.

For example, consider the package

```
package STACK is                        -- specification

     -- This package implements a conventional simple pushdown
     -- stack for items. PUSH and POP operations are provided
     -- with the usual meanings. A maximum of 100 items can
     -- be stored. A fixed amount of memory is used, so neither
     -- dynamic memory allocation nor garbage collection is
     -- needed. Due to the simple data structure, the stack
     -- operations have high performance. An exception is raised
     -- on overflow or underflow. No other exceptions should
     -- occur. No portability problems are envisaged. ITEM type
     -- must be known.

     procedure PUSH(X : in ITEM);
     procedure POP(Y : out ITEM);
     OVERFLOW, UNDERFLOW : exception;

end STACK;                              -- end specification

package body STACK is                   -- body

     MAX : constant := 100;
     S : array(1 .. MAX) of ITEM;
     TOP : NATURAL range 0 .. MAX := 0;

     procedure PUSH(X : in ITEM) is
     begin
          if TOP = MAX then
               raise OVERFLOW;
          end if;
          TOP := TOP + 1;
          S(TOP) := X;
     end PUSH;

     procedure POP(Y : out ITEM) is
     begin
          if TOP = 0 then
               raise UNDERFLOW;
          end if;
          Y := S(TOP);
          TOP := TOP - 1;
     end POP;

end STACK;                              -- end body
```

Users of PUSH and POP are prevented by the rules of the language from making use of the way this STACK is implemented. Thus, providing the specification is unaffected, the implementation of the stack could be changed (e.g. from an array to a linked list) simply by substituting another package body, and the rest of the program would not be affected. Moreover the new body could be brought in as an off-the-shelf software component. Thus Ada packages provide the basis for reusability of software components.

(iv) Package providing abstract data types

Each object of a type possesses a value, one of a set characteristic of the type, and can participate in a set of operations defined for objects of that type. Type definitions (see Chapter 3) define new types by specifying only the value sets: packages may be used to associate such definitions with definitions of the relevent operations, so providing complete type definitions.

The above stack is restricted, in that only one stack object is created by the package declaration. The effect of an abstract data type, from which a number of objects can be created, can be achieved by including a private type in the visible part of the package. The interface subprograms, in this case PUSH and POP, now take the private type as one of their parameters. (In this example, comments are omitted.)

```
package STACKS is

     type STACK is limited private;
     procedure PUSH(S : in out STACK; X : in ITEM);
     procedure POP(S : in out STACK; Y : out ITEM);
     OVERFLOW, UNDERFLOW : exception;
private
     MAX : constant := 100;
     type STACK_STRUCTURE is array(1 .. MAX) of ITEM;
     type STACK is
          record
               TOP : NATURAL range 0 .. MAX := 0;
               STACK_ARRAY : STACK_STRUCTURE:
          end record;

end STACKS;
```

Stack objects must be declared and they will be initialized by the default initialization to be empty. Thus:

```
STACK1, STACK2 : STACK;
...
STACKS.PUSH(STACK1, A);          -- use of STACK1
```

The concept of the private type is central to this kind of data abstraction, since it allows a type to be named without revealing its implementation details. A generic type parameter can be used to provide the ability to declare stacks with different element types (see 12c).

(v) Package providing abstract data types with discriminants

When it is deemed necessary to give users of the package the possibility to adjust the maximum stack size, it can be done in the following way (comments omitted):

```
package STACKS is

     type STACK(SIZE : NATURAL := 100) is limited private;
     procedure PUSH(S : in out STACK; X : in ITEM);
     procedure POP(S : in out STACK; Y : out ITEM);
     OVERFLOW, UNDERFLOW : exception;
private
     type STACK_STRUCTURE is array(NATURAL range <>) of ITEM;
     type STACK(SIZE : NATURAL := 100) is
          record
               TOP : NATURAL := 0;
               STACK_ARRAY : STACK_STRUCTURE(1 .. SIZE);
          end record;

end STACKS;
```

Now one can declare stack objects such as

```
STACK1, STACK2 : STACK;
STACK3         : STACK(1000);
```

The stacks STACK1 and STACK2 can contain 100 items at most, while STACK3 can contain 1000 items.

(vi) Package as parameterless generic.

Generics without any formal parameters may be used to obtain a similar effect to the package STACKS (i.e. to create collections of identical stack objects), but making matters simpler for the user. The specification (without comments) is

```
generic
package STACK is
```

```
        procedure PUSH(X : in ITEM);
        procedure POP(Y : out ITEM);
        OVERFLOW, UNDERFLOW : exception;

    end STACK;
```

Initialization can be handled by the body, so that objects need only be instantiated before use, and calling is simpler for the user:

```
    package STACK1 is new STACK;
    package STACK2 is new STACK;
    ...
    STACK1.PUSH (A);                    -- use of STACK1
```

(vii) Package containing tasks

Tasks may be included in a package body for two main reasons. They may be required to synchronize operations provided by the package, or they may be enclosed in a package to permit them to be treated as library objects. These uses are discussed in chapters 9 and 10.

The rules that follow provide general guidance for the structuring of programs into packages, but the discussion following them indicates that a compromise is frequently necessary when deciding on the details of the structuring. For detailed discussion of many of the compromises involved, with extensive examples, see [Hibbard 1981].

a) The structuring into packages should be based on the identification of abstractions appropriate to the problem.

Details of the implementation of an abstraction should be hidden within the package.

b) A logical hierarchy of packages should be used to reflect or model levels of abstraction.

When abstractions have a hierarchical relationship, the packages implementing them should be built as a logical hierarchy. Note that such a hierarchy tends to be built bottom up. For example, software for a graphics terminal will at a low level have a package for the basic operations such as line drawing. At the next level there will be packages for drawing objects such as rectangles.

c) A package should be used to collect related pieces of information.

Information can be related through common use. Whenever two or more subprograms share some information, there is a possible candidate for a package. The suitability of this candidate should be assessed in view of the following rules and relevant discussion.

d) Related data and operations should be collected in a package.

A named collection of declarations, such as WORK_DATA in 7(i), will usually be associated with operations defined elsewhere in the program. The possibility of restructuring the program to place them with the types and data on which they operated should be considered.

e) Packages should be used to hide machine dependencies.

This strengthens rule c if the information concerned is machine dependent. See Portability Guide 7, 9.8, 13 and 14.

f) Packages should be used defensively.

An important purpose of packages is to prevent users from seeing what they need not see, but a consequent danger is that the user may be constrained to use a package inefficiently in some cases because the user is denied the opportunity of making use of knowledge of package implementation details. (For example, a package for complex arithmetic can be implemented either with cartesian representation or the polar equivalent. The arithmetic operations will have very different performance characteristics. When choosing between different packages, such general performance characteristics must be known. See 7.1b.)

g) Packages should be robust.

Package interfaces should be designed so that their internal operation cannot be sabotaged by misuse. However, it should also be noted that making a package overly robust for its use in a particular context may lead to inefficiencies.

h) Package interfaces should be simple.

Simplicity both in the number of interfaces within a system and in the specification of each is a hallmark of good design. Coupling between a package and other system components should be minimized [Page-Jones 1980]. This means that the number of interfaces (visible procedures, functions, etc.) and the information conveyed in the parameters should be as small as possible. For example a structure should not be provided as a parameter when only one component of the structure is needed. If interfaces appear complicated, the program design should be examined; the boundary for the package may have been badly chosen.

i) For reusability, a package should be made as general as possible if this does not decrease its usefulness for the primary purpose.

Designing a package as a software component encourages adherence to the above rules. But generality in packages and simplicity in their interfaces can lead to inefficiency in particular cases.

j) Lexical nesting of a package should not normally be used to obtain access to objects local to the containing unit.

Such nesting restricts the use of a package as a generally available component. In certain circumstances this is desirable. A comment should be given in the package specification giving the reason for the nesting (whether to obtain access to objects outside or to restrict the accessability of the package or both).

The above rules summarize the main ideas about the use of Ada packages. The following rules concern use of some particular constructs within packages.

7.1 Package Structure

a) The specification should be short and correctly annotated.

Succinctness (see 1.7d) and correctness of comment (see 2.7d) are particularly important as there may be many readers of the specification. A short specification is desirable in as much as it reflects a simple user interface, and implementation detail is excluded.

b) The specification should be complete, both from a semantic and syntactic point of view.

The syntactic information is used both by the programmer using the package and by the compiler. The semantic information is used by the programmer using the package and should describe what the package does, and properties of the package, including performance characteristics, memory usage (dynamic memory, garbage collection, etc.) and operations that have the INLINE pragma.

Note that comment is always necessary to complete the semantic information for a package providing operations. (It is beyond the scope of this document to suggest the best method of providing the semantic information. The reader is referred to [Abbott & Booch 1982] and [Krieg-Brueckner *et al*. 1982].

The interface required by the Ada language concerns how the package appears to the user in normal use. Other forms of communication may not be obvious from the package specification unless included in comment. The package may access global variables. The package may have side effects. There may be language defined exceptions or exceptions declared outside the package which can be raised within the package. The package may contain abort statements to abort tasks in the calling program. The package may contain tasks which could be aborted by the calling program. All such forms of communication which could arise for a package should be mentioned in its specification in comment.

Lastly, the comment should include information about any requirements of the package from its environment, and so, for example, whether any portability problems may arise (see Portability Guide Chapter 7). External packages used by the package but not mentioned in a 'with' clause immediately preceding the package should be named in the comment. Any other information imported by the package (for example the data type information about ITEM imported by the package STACK in 7(iii)) should be included.

c) The private part of a package specification should only be used to supply the full definitions of private types and deferred constants; all other declarations should be put in the package body.

The intention of this rule is to avoid having to recompile dependent packages when these declarations are changed.

d) Careful attention should be paid to the provision of constant values by a package.

When a package wants to export a constant, either a function can return the constant value or the value can be set within the package specification for direct use by the rest of the program. The stack example contains a constant MAX which specifies the stack size. To export this size one could either add

```
function STACK_SIZE return NATURAL;
```

or

```
STACK_SIZE : constant := 100;
```

to the specification part. With the former, the stack size can be changed in the package without the need for change or even recompilation of the program(s) using the package. (The calling overhead can sometimes be avoided if the 'inline' pragma is specified (but then recompilation may be needed.) With the latter, all users of the package can take advantage of the knowledge about the stack size. It can be part of compile-time or static expressions, and other data objects can be given sizes matching this size. On the other hand, if the stack size is changed, all programs using the package must be recompiled. Note also that the latter choice permits the value to be used in a case statement, which is not possible for the result of a function.

e) The package identifier should be repeated at the end of the package specification and body (if any).

7.3 Package Bodies

a) Calls from the "sequence of statements" constituting the initialization code for a package, to functions or procedures not locally defined, should be avoided.

Such a call prevents elaboration of the package declaration if the body of the called unit is not yet elaborated. It therefore restricts freedom in the order of compilation of the library units.

7.4.1 Private Types

a) Private types should be used when it is unnecessary or undesirable for the user to know how the values of his objects are represented.

Private types prevent misuse of structures by users, presenting them only with the abstract operations appropriate for the abstractions involved. A penalty is the need to provide special operations to construct values. Note that values of a private type cannot be composed from their elements by the use of aggregates.

Private types provide an important method of information hiding. As much as possible of the implementation detail should be hidden in the body of the package. It is worthwhile using a private type (as opposed to a record type for example) when this detail (i.e. the "representation" of the type) might change.

b) Objects of private type should be initialized by default if possible.

Because the user does not know how the type is implemented, it may not be possible to initialize objects correctly. The initialization should be performed within the package.

7.4.4 Limited Types

a) Limited types should be used where predefined equality or assignment is inappropriate, or might produce unexpected results.

With complicated data structures the semantics of equality are often unclear. For example, where a stack is defined as a record type as in 7(iv) and 7(v), equality could have at least three different meanings:

(i) The stacks are actually a single object, and the stacks occupy the same storage cells.
(ii) The stack areas have the same content throughout.
(iii) The stacks have the same number of elements currently stored, and the corresponding elements have the same values.

If the STACK type in 7(iv) and 7(v) had not been given as limited private, the predefined equality operator would have been available with the meaning (ii) above, such that two stacks would only be equal if their TOPs are equal and the contents of entire stack space was equal (and some locations may have been neither initialized nor written into). This seems very inappropriate, hence the use of limited private. If equality is required, it should be expicitly defined with suitable semantics.

b) Limited private types should be used for control over private information or resources.

Because of the lack of the predefined assignment, the ability of a user to copy objects can be controlled by the writer of the package. The example of LRM 7.4.4 shows how the number of objects generated from a type can be limited; in this case a limit of 200 is set. Such cases are likely to occur in systems which either are highly secure or require the allocation of restricted resources.

8

Visibility rules

a) The scope of identifiers should not extend further than necessary.

The scope of any declaration should span as small a region of text as possible, in order to limit the amount of information that the reader has to remember and to maximize the defence against accidental use of the identifier outside that scope. See 1.71.

A declaration should be close in the text before its first use. The end of scope should be close in the text after its last use. Program units should be as small as possible, but without excessive fragmentation.

Where a scope is extended by 'with' clauses, these clauses should cover as small a region of text as possible. It is possible to remove a section of text from a unit so that the section has certain global variables visible, but the unit does not. This is achieved by the use of subunits which can have different 'with' clauses from their parents.

b) Redefinition of an identifier in different declarations should be avoided.

The ambiguity caused by redeclaration of an identifier is likely to cause confusion. However this rule should not be used as an excuse to keep the same identifier while changing its meaning; a variable should not be used for one purpose and then another.

An exception to this rule can be made for mathematical computations when variables like x or y may be declared in different declarations as auxiliary variables.

c) Qualified expressions should be used where applicable.

In cases where the context gives sufficient information for qualification to be avoided, it is recommended that the qualification is made where this will help the reader.

8.4 Use Clauses

a) The 'use' clause should only be used to avoid excessive appearance of a package name.

Identifiers made directly visible by the 'use' clause may cause some problems of resolution. The reader may have difficulty in finding the source of identifiers. (Note that suitable cross-reference tools may be available and so alleviate this problem.) Furthermore, some identifier that the reader might expect to become directly visible may not, either because of the same identifier occurring in the source text of the user program, or because the same identifier has been imported from another package.

An excessive use of selected components may be avoided by using renaming declarations. Similarly packages with long names can be renamed with short names to avoid cluttering the text of the user program. However, any shortened forms of package name should be meaningful. If the dot notation substantially reduces readability, the 'use' clause is preferable.

b) The 'use' clause should follow the 'with' clause, unless this extends the scope of the 'use' clause unnecessarily.

8.6 The Package Standard

a) Items from the package STANDARD should not be redefined, without good reason.

b) The package STANDARD should not be named in a 'with' clause.

This would be redundant.

9

Tasks

Tasks are program units which behave like separate programs, running concurrently with others. Concurrency permits a task to await some event, or the expiry of some delay, without affecting the operation of other tasks.

The use of tasks allows the programmer to separate his concern for defining the action to be done from the scheduling of its execution in relation to other actions.

Tasks may not be independent library units, but are declared internally to some other program unit. This may be a procedure, a function, a package or another task.

Tasks have three main purposes:

(i) They may model or control co-existing objects in the problem domain.

Consider a bank with clerks, tellers, cashiers, and customers, each going about his business, more or less independently and concurrently with others, though from time to time they may interact. A clerk may be idle, waiting for the arrival of a customer, for example.

In a computer model of the bank, the model of a clerk may be as follows:

```
task BANK_CLERK is
     entry GIVE_SERVICE( ... );
end BANK_CLERK;
```

```
task body BANK_CLERK is
begin
     loop
          accept GIVE_SERVICE( ... ) do
               ...    -- Perform necessary actions.
          end GIVE_SERVICE;
          ...
     end loop;
end BANK_CLERK;
```

In general such tasks spend much of their time performing actions in persuit of their objectives.

(ii) They may serve as controlling and synchronizing agents, providing the effects of semaphores and locks, buffers, monitors, agents and schedulers, controlling access to shared resources, or synchronizing the actions of otherwise independent tasks.

A typical task to protect a shared data structure from simultaneous reading and writing has the form:

```
task RESOURCE_PROTECTION is
     entry READ(X : out DATUM);
     entry WRITE(X : in  DATUM);
end RESOURCE_PROTECTION;

task body RESOURCE_PROTECTION is
     ITEM : DATUM;                 -- Declare protected variable
                                   -- of type DATUM.
     STARTED : BOOLEAN := FALSE;
                                   -- To ensure that no read is
                                   -- accepted before a write.
begin
     loop
          select  when STARTED =>
               accept READ(X : out DATUM) do
                    X := ITEM;
               end READ;
          or
               accept WRITE(X : in DATUM) do
                    ITEM := X;
               end WRITE;
               STARTED := TRUE;
          or
               terminate;
          end select;
     end loop;
end RESOURCE_PROTECTION;
```

This type of task spends most of its time waiting on entry calls by the active tasks it controls.

(iii) Finally, tasks may serve to define concurrent algorithms for faster execution on multiprocessor architectures (see 9e).

a) Tasks should be used only where they are required to fulfil one of the three roles described above.

Undue complexity of task structures should be avoided. Tasks which mix roles of active and synchronizing tasks violate the generally desirable practice of separating functionality (action) from control.

b) Active tasks should interact in a user/server relationship or in a producer/consumer relationship.

Tasks communicate through entry calls. This relationship is asymmetric, and should be exploited to construct tasks in a user server relationship.

```
task BANK_CUSTOMER is ...
task body BANK_CUSTOMER is
begin
    ...
    BANK_CLERK.GIVE_SERVICE( ... );
    ...
end BANK_CUSTOMER;
```

(See 9.21 for a more complex example.)

Tasks communicating as equals should normally do so through a data buffer. One task 'produces' items which are inserted into the buffer, while the other 'consumes' items, removing them from the buffer as it requires them. The buffer must be protected by a synchronizing task against simultaneous access by the tasks which use it, and ensuring correct behaviour when the buffer is full or empty. See, for example, [Downes & Goldsack 1983] page 151.

Note that user/server and producer/consumer relationships are not restricted to one-to-one.

c) Comments should be included to show the role played in a program by each task.

d) Finite composite actions should be expressed as tasks enclosed in a procedure.

A call on a procedure enclosing a task or tasks, may model an execution of a collection of finite, logically concurrent actions which can be conceived as a single (finite) composite action.

The following example is due to V. A. Downes [Downes & Goldsack 1982]:

```
procedure COOK_DINNER is
     task BOIL_POTATOES;
     task ROAST_MEAT;
     task MAKE_SALAD;
     task body BOIL_POTATOES is separate;
     task body ROAST_MEAT    is separate;
     task body MAKE_SALAD    is separate;
begin
     null;
end COOK_DINNER;
```

A special case is tasks declared in the main program, itself a procedure. These model the life of the entire system, regarded as a single composite action.

e) Algorithms to evaluate complicated functions using parallelism may be defined by tasks enclosed in a function, but they should only be so used when appropriate.

Such parallelism may introduce overheads, if used on an unsuitable architecture.

f) All tasks enclosed in functions or procedures must terminate automatically.

A procedure or function containing tasks cannot return to the calling program until all its dependent tasks have terminated. Such tasks must therefore terminate either by reaching the 'end', or through the operation of a selective wait statement with a terminate alternative (see 9.4).

g) Tasks enclosed in packages should be used to model concurrent behaviour of co-existing objects.

To model or control system components which exist throughout the life of the system, tasks in the main program may suffice. To create independently compilable units, or to restrict visibility of such tasks to the rest of the program, they must be enclosed in packages.

There is no need for such a task to terminate in the normal course of its actions. It may loop forever, maintaining the illusion of a continuous model. See, however, 9.4b and 9.10 for provision for termination on system close-down.

A package may contain several task declarations, generally arranged with the specification parts of all the tasks preceding any body. This permits the model to allow for interactions between any pair of the tasks. In such structures the bodies may be declared 'separate'.

```
package P is                          -- Package specification
    ...
end P;

package body P is                     -- body

    task T1 is
         entry INITIALIZE;
         entry READ_DATA(X : out DATUM);     -- Entries of T1.
    end T1;

    task T2 is
         entry INITIALIZE;
         entry READ_DATA(X : out DATUM);     -- Entries of T2.
    end T2;
    task body T1 is separate;
    task body T2 is separate;
          -- Both bodies see both specifications.
begin

    T1.INITIALIZE;       -- Calls to initialize the
    T2.INITIALIZE;       -- tasks.

end P;                  -- end body
```

This type of structure is appropriate to model a 'subsystem' of closely coupled units.

Units with more independence are better modelled as independent packages. Judgement must be used: do the objects modelled exist concurrently, but constitute independent subsystems? If so they are better enclosed in separate packages.

Consider the following:

```
package P1 is
     ...
end P1;

package P2 is
     ...
end P2;

package body P1 is
     ...
end P1;

with P1;
package body P2 is
     ...
end P2;
```

The tasks are declared in the bodies of the packages. Control of the possible interactions between the units can now be handled in a more refined way by the use of the 'with' clauses. In the example as given here, 'with' clauses are given so that the package body of P2 'sees' the specification of P1.

It is however, still necessary to decide what to make visible in the package specifications. If the task specification is declared in the package visible part

```
package P1 is

     task T1 is
          entry INITIALIZE;
          entry READ_DATA(X : out DATUM);
     end T1;

end P1;
```

then the visibility is just as it was when the task was in the same unit. In this example, the task has an entry to handle its initialization, to be called by the initializing code during the elaboration of the package. It does not seem appropriate to make that entry public. It may not even be desirable to let the rest of the program see that there is a task there. Such units may be given a procedural interface, with procedure names for those entries which are relevant to the rest of the program. The bodies of these procedures may then call the relevant task entries (see 9.5).

h) It should not be assumed that a terminate alternative in a select statement will have any effect for a task enclosed in a package (see 9.4b).

i) Tasks enclosed in a package should be used to implement a protected data-structure (monitor) with local scope when other associated declarations (e.g. types for the parameters) are required.

For example:

```
package PROTECTED_RESOURCE is

    type DATUM is ...
    task RESOURCE_PROTECTION is
        entry READ(X : out DATUM);
        entry WRITE(X : in  DATUM);
    end RESOURCE_PROTECTION;

end PROTECTED_RESOURCE;
```

The task body defined in the package body is identical with that in rule a above.

j) If a resource is to be protected with a more sophisticated protocol than simple mutual exclusion, then a procedural interface must be used, with the task specification hidden in the body.

For the example of readers and writers, where one writer or any number of readers are permitted simultaneous access to the data, see [Barnes 1983] p222. Such tasks should always have terminate alternatives.

9.1 Task Specifications and Task Bodies

a) In a given declarative part, all task specification parts should appear before any task body.

b) Task bodies should be made separate, unless they are quite small.

In the program text, bodies must appear in the same declarative part, following the specifications. However, they do not have to follow immediately. It is usually preferable to declare all the task specifications first, followed by the bodies, so giving all bodies visibility of all the specifications. Bodies may be declared as separate. This helps to keep the module size small, and enable finer control over visibility (see 10.1.1c).

c) No assumptions should be made concerning the relative order of execution of the code of a program unit, and the execution of any task which it may contain.

A task dependent on a program unit is created on elaboration of that unit and starts executing at the 'begin' of the unit body definition (or where the begin might be, in the case of a package with null initializing code). The task then executes in parallel with the code of the unit. This has special consequences when the unit is a package, in which case the code is normally the initialization code for the unit. If there is a data-structure used by the task, which must be initialized, saoy a queue set to empty, then this may be done at the declaration of th structure:

```
package body P is
     X : STRUCTURE := ...    -- Initial values
     task T is
          ...
begin                        -- These two lines
     null;                   -- may be omitted.
end P;
```

The alternative

```
package body P is

     X : STRUCTURE;
     task T is
          ...
begin
     X := ...                -- Initial values

end P;
```

may malfunction, since the task may use the structure before it is initialized.

d) If the initialization of the data structure is so complex as to be impracticable without an algorithm of several steps, then a rendezvous should be used to signal its completion to the task.

For example, in the following, the entry T.START will be called once during the elaboration of the package:

```
package body P is

     X : STRUCTURE;

     task T is
          entry START;
          ...                -- Other entries.
     end T;

     task body T is
     begin
          accept START;
          ...
     end T;
begin
     ...                     -- Initialize X.
     T.START;

end P;
```

9.2 Task Types and Task Objects

a) To avoid the introduction of unnecessary names, directly named tasks (tasks with anonymous task types) should be used whenever a single instance of the task type is all that is required.

Tasks may be unique named tasks, specified by task declarations. In the context of a game, for example, there is a single umpire.

```
task UMPIRE is
     ...
end UMPIRE;
task body UMPIRE is ... etc.
```

On the other hand there are usually many players. In a game of bridge, one of the players (NORTH) might be specified in a task declaration of the form:

```
task NORTH is
     ...                    -- Entry specifications
end NORTH;
task body NORTH is ... etc.
```

A separate definition would then be needed for each of the other players. Since each obeys the same rules, it is better to derive them all from a common definition.

b) Objects of task types should be used whenever several program units have the same behaviour.

Tasks may be derived from a task type definition:

```
task type BRIDGE_PLAYER is
     ...                    -- Entry specifications.
end BRIDGE_PLAYER;
task body BRIDGE_PLAYER is ... etc.
```

The latter may then be followed by the definition of objects of the type, in a declaration:

```
NORTH : BRIDGE_PLAYER;
```

which produces exactly the same effect as before. However, the task type definition permits a number of more powerful extensions.

c) Identical tasks should be derived from a common task type.

For example:

```
JOHN, MARY, JACK, JILL : BRIDGE_PLAYER;
```

d) To associate a task with others tasks, or to associate a task with data, variables of task type may be included as elements of data-structures.

Tasks in records may model clusters of logically associated tasks, or associate tasks with data; an array of tasks may be appropriate to model collections of identical processes, such as the bridge players in the above example. Thus:

```
type POSITION is (NORTH, SOUTH, EAST, WEST);
BRIDGE_GAME : array(POSITION) of BRIDGE_PLAYER;
```

e) To invoke an action involving some selected member of the set of tasks derived from a common type, variables of task type may be passed as parameters to procedures or functions or entry calls.

Thus:

```
procedure PLAY(X : in BRIDGE_PLAYER);
```

may be called with

```
PLAY(MARY);
```

or with

```
PLAY(BRIDGE_GAME(NORTH));
```

f) Static task structures should be used whenever they are sufficient.

In the foregoing examples, JOHN and BRIDGE_TABLE(SOUTH) are immutably associated with particular instances of the task type. It would not be possible for John and Mary to change hands, to let John play out the dummy, for example. Also, the total number of tasks is constant, one for each variable of the type. The tasks are said to be static.

g) Access variables of types suitable for naming tasks should be used when it is essential to create and destroy tasks dynamically, or to be able to change the names with which they are associated.

For example, tasks may be named by access variables:

```
type PLAYER_NAME is access BRIDGE_PLAYER;
JOHN, MARY, JILL, JACK : PLAYER_NAME;
```

The names are now suitable for naming instances of the type, but are at present undefined. They become defined by statements of the form:

```
JOHN := new BRIDGE_PLAYER;
MARY := new BRIDGE_PLAYER;
```

They can be associated with different tasks at different times. This would allow the players to move to different playing positions. For example, to allow John to take over Mary's hand, the assignment

```
JOHN := MARY;
```

might be sufficient. In this case JOHN'S old hand has become anonymous, while MARY is a second name for the same hand.

h) Duplicate names for a task should be avoided, unless it is required by the underlying model.

In general, aliases in a program are undesirable, since they may make the program less clear. It may not be obvious that an action on a named object changes the object named by its alias. A particularly dangerous situation arises if a task is aborted and its name assigned to some other task. Any other name for the aborted task is left 'dangling', and its use would lead to an erroneous program.

Having JOHN and MARY name the same task could have been avoided in the above by setting MARY to null:

```
JOHN := MARY;
MARY := null;
```

or by arranging to swap the values, so that MARY takes JOHN's hand, and vice versa:

```
declare
     TEMP : BRIDGE_PLAYER;
begin
     TEMP := MARY;
     MARY := JOHN;
     JOHN := TEMP;
end;
```

i) Unterminated tasks should not normally be made anonymous.

An anonymous task cannot be named to abort it, and so it could become a useless overhead in the system. Space and machine cycles for its execution may continue to be consumed so long as the task remains unterminated. The garbage collector cannot delete an active task.

j) Records which associate access variables with tasks, should be used to construct linked lists of tasks, to model collections of indefinite size.

For example:

```
type LIST_ELEMENT;
type LIST is access LIST_ELEMENT;
type LIST_ELEMENT is
     record
          NAME : BRIDGE_PLAYER;
          NEXT : LIST;
     end record;
```

Note that the access variable in this case is not of task type.

k) Task types with access variables should be used to permit dynamic generation of tasks during program execution.

In general the access variable is appropriate when it is necessary to associate a name temporarily with a particular instance of a task; the name will be given to a different instance of the task type at a later time.

1) Task types with access variables to name them should be used to enable a task to store its own identity, or to pass it to other tasks, enabling the cooperating task to call back.

This is the appropriate technique when several tasks of common type may call an entry, and the server task needs to know which made a particular call, and the calling tasks are not members of an array. (See 9.2o below.)

The following declarations might occur in a program unit called EXAMPLE:

```
type USER;                  -- Incomplete declaration
                            -- for visibility.

type USER_NAME is access USER;

task type USER is
     entry RECEIVE_REPLY(X : in ... );
     entry INITIALIZE(NAME : in USER_NAME);
     ...
end USER;
task SERVER is              -- Just one server
     entry DO_MY_JOB(NAME : in USER_NAME; X : in ... );
     ...
end SERVER;

task body USER   is separate;
task body SERVER is separate;

JOHN, MARY: USER_NAME;
```

At a later point in the program the bodies are declared:

```
separate (EXAMPLE)
task body USER is
     ME : USER_NAME;
begin
     accept INITIALIZE(NAME : in USER_NAME) do
          ME := NAME;          -- User stores his identity.
     end INITIALIZE;
     ...
     ...
     SERVER.DO_MY_JOB(ME, ... );    -- Give identity
                                    -- to server.
     ...                            -- continue actions.
     accept RECEIVE_REPLY( ... );
     ...
end USER;
```

```
separate (EXAMPLE)
task body SERVER is
    BOSS: USER_NAME;
begin
    accept DO_MY_JOB(NAME : in USER_NAME; X : in ... ) do
        BOSS := NAME;              -- Store user's identity
    end DO_MY_JOB;
    ...                            -- Perform service
    ...
    BOSS.RECEIVE_REPLY(X : in ... );
                                   -- Reply to appropriate user
    ...
end SERVER;
```

Within the scope of these declarations, task instances may be created:

```
JOHN := new USER;
MARY := new USER;

JOHN.INITIALIZE(JOHN);
MARY.INITIALIZE(MARY);
```

JOHN and MARY now each call the server, and receive the appropriate replies. They do not have to wait for completion of the action by the server when there is some concurrent action they can do.

m) Dynamic generation of tasks should only be used when appropriate.

Appropriate use is to model objects which enter and leave the system, such as the users of a computer system.

Generation of messenger tasks, which queue at a common entry to a destination task is a way of implementing a 'no-wait send' with unbounded buffering between communicating tasks (violating rule 9.2j). It is not recommended as a normal programming technique; such buffering is better provided by a linked list (of records containing tasks). It may, however, have a role in programming distributed systems.

Consider the following declarations:

```
OUTGOING: MESSAGE;

task type M;
task body M is
     LOCAL : MESSAGE := OUTGOING;
begin
     DESTINATION.RECEIVE(LOCAL);
end;

type M_NAME is access M;

procedure ASYNCH_SEND(X : in MESSAGE) is
     MM : M_NAME;
begin
     OUTGOING := X;
     MM := new M;
end ASYNCH_SEND;
```

Within the scope of these declarations, a call on the procedure ASYNCH_SEND causes elaboration of a new instance of the task type M, automatically initialising LOCAL to the value of the message. The task then calls the entry in the destination task. This may be made generic, as described in chapter 12, with both the message type and the destination entry being parameters.

This form is both simple and elegant, and minimises the time which the calling task must lose in preparing and sending the message. It is insufficient, however, if it is to be called by several tasks. The variable OUTGOING is then shared, and malfunction is possible if a task reschedule occurs after the assignment to OUTGOING, and before the elaboration of the new instance of the messenger task. It is possible to make ASYNCH_SEND into a task entry, making the two instructions indivisible, but in that case the calling task may suffer some delay in the entry call. In that case the following solution is preferred:

```
task type MESSENGER is
     entry CONVEY_MESSAGE(X : in MESSAGE);
end MESSENGER;
```

```
task body MESSENGER is
     SCROLL : MESSAGE;
begin
     accept CONVEY_MESSAGE(X : in MESSAGE) do
          SCROLL := X;
     end CONVEY_MESSAGE;
     DESTINATION.RECEIVE(SCROLL);
end MESSENGER;

type MESSENGER_TYPE is access MESSENGER;
ACHILLES : MESSENGER_TYPE;
```

New messenger tasks may be repeatedly created to convey messages to some destination, without concern for whether they arrive safely, by repeated executions of a program sequence:

```
ACHILLES := new MESSENGER;
ACHILLES.CONVEY_MESSAGE(LATEST);
```

If for any reason, the destination task should fail to accept entry calls, then this scheme will lead to a proliferation of anonymous messenger tasks. (Only the most recent instance will be accessible as ACHILLES).

The tasks will not terminate normally until their calls are accepted, and it is not possible to abort them explicitly - only indirectly by aborting the task in which they are created (see rule 9.2i).

The presence of large numbers of such inaccessible tasks is likely to cause overheads in scheduling and storage, and to hinder the checking of programs.

n) An array of objects of task type may be used to create a set of equivalent units, modelling a collection of similar items in the problem domain.

o) When a task, a member of a collection of related tasks, needs to be able to identify itself to a partner, it must know its own identity. This should be supplied in the form of its index or access name, supplied as a parameter during a special entry, called once during the initialization. (See also 9.2l.)

Consider for example, the collection of lifts serving a building. The lifts do not know their identity, unless they are told it.

```
package LIFT_SYSTEM is

     type LIFT_INDEX is range 1 .. MAX_LIFTS;

end LIFT_SYSTEM;

package body LIFT_SYSTEM is

     task type LIFT is
          entry START(N : in LIFT_INDEX);
     end LIFT;

     task body LIFT is
          X : LIFT_DATA       -- Data modelling the lift.
          LIFT_NUMBER : LIFT_INDEX;
     begin
          accept START(N : in LIFT_INDEX) do
               LIFT_NUMBER := N;
          end START;
          ...                 -- The real "life" of the lift.
     end LIFT;
     LIFT_SET : array(LIFT_INDEX) of LIFT;
begin
     for L in LIFT_INDEX loop
          LIFT_SET(L).START(L);
     end loop;

end LIFT_SYSTEM;
```

Here the initialization code starts all the lifts, and tells each its identity.

p) Data which logically belongs to a task should be made local to it, rather than associated with it in a record.

An object of task type may be included in a record. If a program is written using this structure to associate data with the task to which it logically belongs, as in the following example:

```
type LIFT_UNIT is record
   X : LIFT_DATA;
   L : LIFT;
end record;
```

The task L does not automatically see its associated data. Thus, an array of these objects:

```
LIFT_CLUSTER : array(1 .. MAX_LIFTS) of LIFT_UNIT;
```

must still be initialized to tell each lift its number, and from within its own body it would still have to access its own data with

```
LIFT_CLUSTER(LIFT_NUMBER).X
```

q) Data associated with a task in a record should be used to model information about the object which is intended for use by other system components.

For example:

```
task type VEHICLE is ...
type VEHICLE_INSTANCE is record
     ACTIVE_UNIT  : VEHICLE;
     REGISTRATION : REGISTRATION_NUMBER;
end record;
```

This is a correct use of tasks in records, since the data associated with it, the registration number, is for external use. The data modelling the driver's panel of instruments, for example, would be stored internally to the task.

9.4 Task Dependence - Termination of Tasks

a) A task dependent directly or indirectly on a procedure or a function must terminate by reaching its 'end', or must have a selective wait with a terminate alternative.

The same rule applies to a task dependent on another task which is itself dependent on a function or a procedure.

Note that a task declared in a package which is itself declared internally to another program unit, does not depend on the package, but on that subprogram or library unit which ultimately contains it.

It is important to realize that no unit can terminate until all dependent tasks have terminated. Functions and procedures cannot return to the calling program until all dependent tasks have terminated, so any task calling a subprogram containing a non-terminating task will be indefinitely delayed.

b) Provision should be made for graceful termination of a task dependent on a library package at system close down.

A task dependent on a library package cannot be made to terminate by including a terminate option in a select. There is in fact no need for it to terminate at all. If the main program terminates without closing down tasks in library units which it has created, the consequence is not defined in the LRM. Provision for graceful system close down is preferable. This may be obtained by an entry call causing it to execute an 'exit' statement taking it out of the its eternal loop, so that it reaches the 'end', and so terminates, or it may be aborted by another task (usually the main program).

9.5 Entry Calls and accept statements

a) In the interest of information hiding, where only certain entries of a task are intended to be called by program components outside an enclosing package, it is preferable to place the specification part of the task inside the package body, introducing procedures which in turn call the actual entries.

b) Entries should not be replaced by procedures in this way if they are to be called in conditional or timed entry calls.

See sections 9.7.2 and 9.7.3. Task entries are visible in the normal scope of their declaration. This means that they are visible in the body of the unit on which they depend, and to the bodies of all tasks which are declared in the same declarative part, but after them. (To enable a pair of tasks to call each other's entries, the specification parts must both be declared before either body.) A task declared in a package may have its specification part declared in the visible part of the package. This makes all its entries visible to other program components. A more general case has a procedural interface.

Consider, for example, a package to manage a buffer, handling calls on a disc file. The users of the package are to be able to write to the disc, but not read from it. But an intermediate task manages the writing, reading from the buffer as required. The visible interface is

```
package DISC_FILING is

     type UNIT_RECORD is ...
     procedure WRITE(X : in UNIT_RECORD);

end DISC_FILING;

package body DISC_FILING is

     task BUFFERING is
          entry READ(X : out UNIT_RECORD);
          entry WRITE(X : in  UNIT_RECORD);
     end BUFFERING;

     task DISC_WRITER;

     task body BUFFERING   is separate;
     task body DISC_WRITER is separate;
     procedure WRITE(X : in UNIT_RECORD) is
     begin
          BUFFERING.WRITE(X);
     end;

end DISC_FILING;

separate (DISC_FILING)
task body BUFFERING is
     ...                 -- Declare a queue structure.
     ...                 -- and functions IS_EMPTY and IS_FULL
begin
     loop
          select
               when not IS_EMPTY  =>
                    accept READ(X : out UNIT_RECORD) do
                         X := ...  -- The next item
                         ...       -- Remove next item
                    end READ;
          or
               when not IS_FULL =>
                    accept WRITE(X : in UNIT_RECORD) do
                         ...       -- Set tail of queue = X
                    end WRITE;
          end select;
     end loop;
end BUFFERING;
```

```
                          -- Note  how the separate body can be  given
with  DISC_UNIT;          -- sole access to the DISC_UNIT (see 10.1.1)
separate (DISC_FILING)
task body DISC_WRITER is
          Y : UNIT_RECORD;
begin
     loop
          BUFFERING.READ(Y);
          DISC_UNIT.WRITE(Y);
     end loop;
end DISC_WRITER;
```

This illustrates how entries may be selectively presented to the package interface.

c) A task should not normally call its own entries.

Bodies also 'see' their own entries, but if they try to call them they deadlock.

d) Families of entries are appropriate when the logical structure calls for a collection of closely related queues, holding calls which must be accepted one at a time.

Calls on a single entry are taken in strict order, first in first out. If a programmer wishes to organize his program to handle calls in some other prescribed way, the calls may be parameterized by an entry index, and the task body organized to accept them in the required order. One important case is to provide for queues to be handled with different priorities. This is illustrated in 9.9.

Another illustrative example is the following. We declare

```
type CITIZENSHIP is (HOME_NATIONAL, EEC, OTHER);

task IMMIGRATION_CONTROL is
     entry CHECK_POINT(CITIZENSHIP)(DATA: in PASSPORT_DATA);
end IMMIGRATION_CONTROL;
```

This allows the formation of separate queues for three classes of immigrant. Each will join an appropriate queue with the call:

```
IMMIGRATION_CONTROL.CHECK_POINT
                    (MY_CITIZENSHIP)(MY_PASSPORT_DATA);
```

e) An array of tasks each with a single entry is appropriate if the entries may be called concurrently.

The distinction between these cases lies in the use of a shared resource. In the first case only one of the entry calls must be accepted at a time, because there is a shared database of data on unwanted immigrants.

The alternative to the above, for the case when there is no shared database might be written as follows:

```
task type IMMIGRATION_CONTROL is
     entry CHECK_POINT(DATA : in PASSPORT_DATA);
end;

IMMIGRATION : array(CITIZENSHIP) of IMMIGRATION_CONTROL;
```

An immigrant would then join the appropriate queue for clearance:

```
IMMIGRATION(MY_CITIZENSHIP).CHECK_POINT(MY_PASSPORT_DATA);
```

f) To avoid deadlock, pairs of tasks should not normally call each other, except to produce the effect of co-routines.

Tasks which call each other are in a particularly dangerous relationship with respect to the possibility of deadlock. Nevertheless, a co-routine relationship is often useful, particularly to resolve structure clashes between an input and output.

For example, suppose a series of matrices is to be read from input in column order and then printed by row. It is necessary to store each complete matrix. Thus, within the scope of the declarations:

```
type ROW    is range 1 .. MAXROW;
type COLUMN is range 1 .. MAXCOLUMN;
MATRIX : array(ROW, COLUMN) of ITEM;

task MATRIX_READER is
     entry READ;
end  MATRIX_READER;

task MATRIX_WRITER is
     entry WRITE;
end  MATRIX_WRITER;
```

```
task body MATRIX_READER is
begin
     loop
          select
               accept READ;
               ...
               ...                    -- Read matrix in column order.
               ...
          or
               terminate;
          end select;
          MATRIX_WRITER.WRITE;    -- Call matrix writer.
     end loop;
end  MATRIX_READER;

task body MATRIX_WRITER is
begin
     loop
          select
               accept WRITE;
               ...
               ...                    -- Write matrix in row order.
               ...
          or
               terminate;
          end select;
          MATRIX_READER.READ; -- Call matrix reader.
     end loop;
end  MATRIX_WRITER;
```

The READ operation is started with a call from the body of the creating unit:

```
MATRIX_READER.READ;
```

g) Only those actions should be included in the accept statement which must be completed before the calling task is released from its waiting state.

A common mistake is to include all those actions which must be done as a consequence of the entry call in the critical section within the scope of the 'accept' ... 'end'. This reduces concurrency, unnecessarily preventing the cooperating task from proceeding with its work.

Usually the work that must be done in this critical section is quite small. The steps following the end of the accept statement are still protected from the consequence of other entry calls in the same task.

Since the called task is not usually sharing data with the caller, there is no need to keep the latter waiting. Nevertheless see rule h below.

To enable concurrency of processing with the caller it is usually necessary to save 'in' parameters in local variables.

```
accept RECEIVE_DATA(X : in THING) do
    LOCAL_THING := X;
end RECEIVE_DATA;
...                        -- process LOCAL_THING.
```

permits more concurrency than the alternative:

```
accept RECEIVE_DATA(X : in THING) do
    ...                    -- process X.
end RECEIVE_DATA;
```

h) The values of parameters of mode 'out' must be computed and assigned to the formal parameters before the end of the accept.

This is a consequence of the scope rules for the parameters. All actions must be included in the accept statement which use the formal parameters of the entry.

9.6 Delay Statements, Duration and Time

a) A delay statement should be used to delay a task until a definite time T by the following:

```
delay T - CALENDAR.CLOCK;
```

Remember that a delay statement causes a delay for at least the specified time. The actual restart of the delayed task may be later than intended. In a program intended to loop with a certain periodic time, cumulative drift may be avoided by calculating the intended time of the next cycle, and then using

```
delay TIME_FOR_NEXT_CYCLE - CALENDAR.CLOCK;
```

b) To specify large delays in absolute units, constants should be defined to represent hours and minutes.

For example, within the scope of the following constant declarations:

```
MINUTES : constant := 60.0;
HOURS   : constant := 60.0 * MINUTES;
```

a delay might be specified in the form:

```
7.0 * HOURS + 9.0 * MINUTES + 23.0;
```

c) A delay statement should be used whenever a task must wait for some known duration.

A busy wait (an idle loop) cannot provide a wait of a known duration, and wastes processor cycles.

d) Knowledge of the execution pattern of tasks should not be used to avoid the use of explicit task synchronization.

Where tasks have a fixed, known time pattern, it may be tempting to try to save overheads of an explicit synchronization through an entry call. Such programs will always be difficult to understand and will be prone to malfunction.

e) The delay statement should normally only be used to manage interaction with an external process which works in real time, or to create a task which behaves in a well-defined manner in real time.

9.7.2 <u>Conditional entry calls</u>

a) Conditional entry calls should be used sparingly to avoid unnecessary busy waiting.

An entry call may be placed in a select statement, with an else part which defines an alternative action should the entry not be immediately accepted. This facility is useful if the calling task must not be delayed in view of some other urgent action it must perform. If, however, the calling task will loop round to try again, then this implements a busy wait.

Renaming of a task entry as a procedure will prevent the use of conditional entry calls.

9.7.3 Timed entry calls

a) The consequence of a time-out on an entry call should generally be the raising of an exception, not a loop round to try again.

b) It should not be assumed that a task is fully protected by a time-out, against malfunction of its communicating partner.

Timed entry calls may be used to protect a task against being forever held waiting for a rendezvous with some other task which fails, probably through malfunction, to accept it. Note, however, that the time-out is on the acceptance of the call, not its completion. If an entry is accepted, and the code of the accept statement fails to terminate, the calling task will still wait forever.

Renaming of a task entry as a procedure will prevent the use of timed entry calls.

9.8 Priorities

A priority is assigned to a task by including a PRIORITY pragma in the specification. This provides guidance to the scheduler in the run-time kernel.

a) The PRIORITY pragma should appear in task specifications before any entry declarations, and in the main program before any declarations.

Note that all instances of a task type have the same priority.

b) Only a small number of priority levels should be used.

This will make the program more portable, as well as more

understandable to the reader.

c) Names should be given to the priority levels by declaring a package of constants of predefined type PRIORITY:

```
with SYSTEM;
package PRIORITY_LEVELS is

      IDLING        : constant PRIORITY := 0;
      BACKGROUND    : constant PRIORITY := 1;
      USER_ACTIVITY : constant PRIORITY := 2;
      CRITICAL      : constant PRIORITY := 3;
      SYSTEM        : constant PRIORITY := 4;

end PRIORITY_LEVELS;
```

d) The priority levels used should be spread over the range made available to type PRIORITY in the implementation.

This makes introduction of new priority levels as easy as possible.

e) For any group of related tasks, such as those declared within the same program unit, priorities should be specified either for all, or for none of them.

A task without a PRIORITY pragma has an undefined priority, with a value dependent on the implementation. It cannot be assumed that all such tasks have the same priority; nor that this priority is lower (or higher) than any which is explicitly specified.

f) Undue reliance should not be placed on priorities defined by the pragma PRIORITY, as they influence only the scheduling of tasks by the run-time system.

Entry calls queued at an entry are taken in first-in first-out order, irrespective of priority. (See 9.9.)

g) Address clauses should not be given for entries not associated with hardware interrupts.

Entries specified with an address clause may be given maximum priority by the system (see 13.5.1). This should not be exploited for entries not associated with hardware interrupts.

9.9 Task and Entry Attributes

Predefined task and entry attribute enquiries enable the current state of a task to be inspected by the program. Care should always be exercised to ensure that any use of such attribute enquiries is valid. It is usually not possible to ensure that the state obtained from the enquiry is unchanged when the decision based on the observation is carried out.

a) The answer FALSE for the T'TERMINATED or TRUE for the T'CALLABLE enquiries should not be trusted.

Use of the T'TERMINATED enquiry may be made to discover if a task is terminated. Presumably this is followed by some action dependent on the result, to avoid the raising of a TASKING_ERROR exception on an entry call, for example. However, this is not secure, since the enquiry and the ensuing call cannot be made an indivisible action. The task may become terminated in the meantime. The answer TRUE is usually safe, but even that may not be if the enquiry is used in an exception handler to discover the cause of the exception, following an error.

b) The E'COUNT enquiry may be used to control the selection from members of a family of entries, to obtain the effect of priority queueing. The following version is not fully safe.

Suppose that within the scope of the type

```
type URGENCY is (HIGH, MEDIUM, LOW);
```

the task is declared:

```
task EXAMPLE is
     entry E(URGENCY);
end EXAMPLE;
```

```
task body EXAMPLE is
begin
  loop
    select
              accept E(HIGH) ...
    or
         when E(HIGH)'COUNT = 0 =>
              accept E(MEDIUM) ...
    or   when E(MEDIUM)'COUNT = 0 and  E(HIGH)'COUNT = 0 =>
              accept E(LOW) ...
    end select;
  end loop;
end EXAMPLE;
```

This is unsafe, unless high priority calls can be guaranteed to be frequent, or to be free from possibility of time-out or abortion. Suppose, when the select statement is entered, E(HIGH)'COUNT = 1. In that case the guards for lower priority calls are closed: only the accept for E(HIGH) is possible. However, it is also possible that the waiting call gets withdrawn at that critical time, either by a time-out, or by abortion of the calling task. In that case lower priority calls are held waiting until a new high priority one arrives to release the task from the select statement. Note that such poor behaviour would probably pass unnoticed in test, as it would not usually lead to total deadlock.

9.10 Abort Statements

a) Abortion of tasks is generally to be avoided.

Abortion involves arbitrary intervention in the actions of one task by another, and could lead to unpredictable results. Nevertheless, it may be appropriate to invoke abortion via a command language, permitting a user to close down part of a system (and perhaps restart it later). It may also be appropriate to invoke abortion within an exception handler in a unit containing subtasks, for example:

```
when others =>
     put("SYSTEM FAILURE");
     abort T1, T2, T3;
end;
```

9.11 Shared Variables

a) Direct sharing of variables between tasks should be avoided.

A pool of shared data may be protected by placing it in a task, and calling read and write entries to access the data. This protects it against simultaneous read and write. This is one of a number of techniques for protecting data (see 9a and 9j).

b) Tasks organized as co-routines may share access to data.

10

Program structure and compilation issues

The structuring of a program into subprograms, packages, tasks and generic units is discussed in Chapters 6, 7, 9 and 12 respectively. The reasons for this structuring include information hiding, data control and abstraction. Some further guidelines on this structuring and on the matter of separate compilation are given below.

a) The structure of an Ada program should not be unduly influenced by concerns of separate compilation.

Ada allows the main issues of program structure to be separated from those of separate compilation. Structuring should be for reasons of information hiding, data control, abstraction and configuration control (see rule d below), etc. Independent of the program structure, parts of the program may be separated from one another for reasons of convenience (see for example rule c) or economy of compilation.

In Ada, program units can be arbitrarily nested or can stand separately from one another. If the units are separated, interdependencies can still be expressed, for example using 'with' clauses.

b) Excessive nesting of subunits should be avoided.

See 1.7n. Subunits are nested only when they wish to use objects declared in an enclosing scope. It is therefore not self-evident from the body of the subunit just what the total effect is. Logical errors may also result from introducing names which do not appear in the scope of the subunit.

Care must therefore be taken if subunits are nested. As a general rule, packages should not be declared inside units other than the "main" program unless thay are being used as a local declaration of an abstract data type object.

c) Program units should be of convenient size for testing.

Small program units when compiled separately can be tested more quickly than larger units or units that have to be compiled together. This is a reason for rule 1.71. However note that excessive fragmentation should be avoided.

d) Library units should be used for purposes of configuration control.

Different configurations of the software may be produced by simply changing one or more library units, without affecting the rest of the software.

10.1 Compilation Units - Library Units

a) Library units providing services to the main program should be packages.

The reason for this rule is to ensure that collections of subprograms are identifiable. However there is a counter argument that such subprograms should be left as separate units in order to facilitate the selective loading of only those subprograms being used by the main program. The compiler implementer might assume that if a package is used then all the subprograms within it should be loaded.

10.1.1 Context Clauses - With Clauses

a) No unit should have a 'with' clause for a unit it does not need to see directly.

Thus scopes of identifiers will not be needlessly extended, and unnecessary compilation dependency is avoided.

Note that, by rules 8.6b and 8.6c, the package STANDARD should never be named in a 'with' or 'use' clause.

b) Parts of a program which depend on a set of external objects should be contained within a single compilation unit.

This means that only one unit has to be recompiled when the specification of those external objects changes.

c) If only a small part of a given unit needs access to a library unit, then it should appear as a subunit and have its own 'with' clause for that library unit.

This reduces dependencies by removing any references to the library unit from the main part of the given unit (see [Barnes 1983] page 115).

10.2 Subunits of Compilation Units

a) Bodies of nested program units should be made separate if they would otherwise reduce the readability of the containing unit, for example by unduly distancing its body from its specification.

10.3 Order of Compilation

a) Excessive dependencies between compilation units should be avoided.

It is important to avoid too much coupling of library units and subunits through 'with' clauses, and in the case of subunits through nesting. Coupling introduces dependencies on compilation order, and complicates and lengthens the recompilation procedure during program maintenance. A complicated network of 'with' clauses probably implies a poorly constructed program. See also 10.1.1a.

b) Tree structures rather than general acyclic graph structures should be used.

To minimize coupling problems, a tree structure should be built where higher level units only depend on lower level units. This is an example of the more general rule 1.7k.

11

Exceptions

The correct use of exceptions can greatly simplify the logic and ease of understanding and use of program components. However, it is certainly true that exceptions are open to misuse. They have been strongly criticized because of this, and although some criticism has been over-severe, nevertheless there are genuine reasons for concern that exceptions be used properly. Unfortunately, there is little experience in the use of exceptions and so the guidelines in this area must be treated as tentative. The fact that exceptions will be new to many programmers is itself a danger. There could be a temptation to over-use them out of misplaced enthusiasm for a new concept.

a) Exceptions should not be used unnecessarily.

As an example of misuse, if type DAY is (MON, TUE, WED, THU, FRI, SAT, SUN), then:

```
begin
     TOMORROW := DAY'SUCC (TODAY);
exception
     when CONSTRAINT_ERROR =>
          TOMORROW := DAY'FIRST;
end;
```

is less straightforward than:

```
if TODAY = DAY'LAST then
     TOMORROW := DAY'FIRST;
else
     TOMORROW := DAY'SUCC (TODAY);
end if;
```

The point is that DAY'LAST, i.e. SUN, is not really exceptional; it occurs regularly and is not surprising.

b) Exceptions should be used for reporting events which are in some sense errors, and thus will not occur in the normal course of events (i.e. in the correct functioning of the system).

A legitimate use of exceptions is illustrated by the package STACK example from 7 (iii), whose specification (without the comments) is

```
package STACK is

     procedure PUSH(X : in ITEM);
     procedure POP(Y : out ITEM);
     OVERFLOW, UNDERFLOW : exception;

end STACK;
```

Overflow or underflow can be generally regarded as being due to an error in the usage of the stack. Overflow may sometimes be due to an error in the dimensioning of the stack; i.e. the stack is not large enough.

c) Exceptions should be used where it can be argued that they are safer (more defensive) than the alternatives, in particular to guard against inadvertent omissions.

For example, if we did not use an exception for the stack error then we would have to test explicitly for the condition on each of PUSH or POP. This implies an additional parameter of type BOOLEAN which is tested after each call. The specification would now become

```
package STACK is

     procedure PUSH(X : in  ITEM;
                    B : out BOOLEAN);
     procedure POP(Y : out ITEM;
                   B : out BOOLEAN);

end STACK;
```

and the user would now write

```
PUSH(A, OK);
if not OK then
...
end if;
```

This illustrates a positive advantage of exceptions. If the user does not provide a handler then the program will terminate. On the other hand, if exceptions are not used and the test of the status value OK has been forgotten, then the program will continue in an incorrect manner and the cause of the error may be difficult to trace when some later symptom arises.

d) Exceptions should be used for reporting events for which it is particularly inconvenient to test at the point of cause/occurrence.

They are of particular value where the event occurs in a deeply nested control structure and is indirectly caused by a call from an outer level.

Suppose the procedures PUSH and POP are used by another more general procedure SLAVE say, and that SLAVE in turn is called in several different places from procedure JOB. Suppose also that if the stack gets misused then the whole call of JOB has to be abandoned. Using exceptions this can be expressed as

```
procedure SLAVE( ... ) is
...
begin
     ...
     PUSH(A);
     ...
     POP(B);
     ...
end;

procedure JOB( ... ) is
...
begin
     ...
     SLAVE( ... );
     ...
     SLAVE( ... );
     ...
exception
     when OVERFLOW =>          -- JOB failed
     ...
end JOB;
```

Using flags we would have to write

```
procedure SLAVE( ... ; OK : out BOOLEAN) is
     ...
begin
     OK := TRUE;
     ...
     PUSH(X, OK);
     if not OK then
          return;
     end if;
     ...
     POP(Y, OK);
     if not OK then
          return;
     end if;
end;

procedure JOB( ... ) is
     OK : BOOLEAN;
     ...
     procedure FAIL is
     begin                                   -- JOB failed
     ...
     end;

begin                                        -- body of JOB
     ...
     SLAVE( ... , OK);
     if not OK then
          FAIL;
          return;
     end if;
     ...
     SLAVE( ... , OK);
     if not OK then
          FAIL;
          return;
     end if;
     ...

end JOB;
```

When using exceptions, the programmer only has to insert one test, namely the appropriate handler. When using flags, the programmer has to insert a test of each call at each level. Note also that the absence of global 'goto's (for obvious reasons of style) means that the return from JOB has to be written out each time and cannot be placed inside the internal procedure FAIL.

It is clear that in such nested situations, the use of exceptions is the neatest solution and therefore less prone to error.

11.1 Exception Declarations

a) The predefined exceptions should be used with care; they should not be relied upon to indicate particular circumstances.

Suppose we omitted to provide our own exception in the package STACK so that it was (without the comment)

```
package STACK is

     procedure PUSH(X : in ITEM);
     procedure POP(Y : out ITEM);

end STACK;

package body STACK is
     ...
     procedure PUSH(X : in ITEM) is
     begin
          TOP := TOP + 1;
          S(TOP) := X;
     end PUSH;
     ...
end STACK;
```

then CONSTRAINT_ERROR will be raised if the stack overflows. The user could then write a handler for CONSTRAINT_ERROR. However, in that handler, there would be no guarantee that the exception has arisen because of misuse of the stack. Something else could have gone wrong in the user's block of code.

The key point is that the predefined exceptions are not usually raised explicitly (of course they can be), and so the possibility of their happening is not textually obvious (see 11.3).

b) Do not explicitly raise an exception in a package outside that package.

Thus in the case of the declared exceptions OVERFLOW and UNDERFLOW we are reasonably assured that they will only be raised in the package STACK. A user should not write

```
with STACK;
procedure BAD is
begin
    ...
    raise STACK.OVERFLOW;
    ...
end;
```

Presumably this could be detected by analysis of the program text. However, for layered recovery, a plain 'raise' statement outside the package is acceptable.

c) Do not rely upon the circumstances causing predefined exceptions without good reasons.

Some of the predefined exceptions need particular care:-

(i) CONSTRAINT_ERROR can occur for a wide variety of reasons. Do not without justification assume a particular reason.

(ii) NUMERIC_ERROR is not to be relied upon if program portability is required. It may or may not be raised according to the implementation.

(iii) STORAGE_ERROR cannot be relied upon in a quantitative manner. The precise conditions which would result in a task or access collection running out of space are implementation dependent.

(iv) TASKING_ERROR generally needs care because of the difficult nature of parallel programming. The precise circumstances in which task communication goes wrong are considerable and it does not seem wise to rely upon TASKING_ERROR to indicate a particular reason.

(v) PROGRAM_ERROR cannot be relied upon. It is only raised when there is an error of a certain kind in the program. Such an error may or may not be detected, depending on the implementation. Exception handlers can be written to help in removing this kind of error from the program during debugging, and may even be left in the final program as an extreme form of defensive programming.

d) Exceptions should not be used as a means of indicating states.

Thus one should not test for an empty stack by calling POP to see whether it raises an exception. An appropriate IS_EMPTY function should be provided in the defining package.

11.2 Exception Handlers

a) The exception choice 'others' should not be used as a shorthand for an anticipated set of exceptions: these exceptions should be written explicitly.

Thus if one anticipates OVERFLOW, UNDERFLOW or NUMERIC_ERROR then one should write

```
when OVERFLOW ! UNDERFLOW ! NUMERIC_ERROR =>
```

and not

```
when others =>
```

The latter will also handle other unexpected exceptions and one may thereby lose information regarding the error.

b) A handler for 'others' may be used to ensure that no exception can be propagated from a unit, and should be used for important tasks.

A task is thus prevented from being inadvertently terminated by its inability to handle an exception, which would not be propagated further. A trivial task such as a buffering task need not have such a handler.

c) The program should be layered such that each layer can raise and handle its own exceptions.

See 1.7k. Each layer should tidy up the state at that layer, for example by closing files opened in that layer and similarly returning other resources acquired by that layer; an exception can then be propagated up to the next layer for further processing if required. However, an exception should be recorded in some way at its original point of handling for later diagnosis; this may require the use of global variables to distinguish different reasons for a common exception.

d) An exception, which cannot be dealt with by some layer, should, if necessary, be converted into an exception that can be explicitly recognized by the next layer, and must not be allowed to propagate outside its own scope.

For example consider

```
function FACTORIAL (N : NATURAL)
        return POSITIVE is
begin
    if N = 0 then
        return 1;
    else
        return N * FACTORIAL (N - 1);
    end if;
end FACTORIAL;
```

Calling FACTORIAL will raise CONSTRAINT_ERROR if the parameter is negative, NUMERIC_ERROR with a moderately large parameter and STORAGE_ERROR with a very large parameter. For general use this function should be encapsulated in a way which handles all these exceptions and propagates some other exception such as FACTORIAL_ERROR.

e) Recursion within an exception handler should be avoided.

Thus if the procedure JOB contains a handler, then JOB should not be called from within that handler to have a further attempt at the execution. If it is desired to recall JOB, then the handler for this should be placed within the calling program.

11.3 Raise Statements

a) The predefined exceptions should not normally be explicitly raised.

A legitimate use might be where NUMERIC_ERROR is raised to indicate some misuse of a mathematical function.

11.7 Suppressing Checks

a) Checks should not be suppressed without good reason.

There is no guarantee that the compiler will suppress the check and in any event the corresponding exception could be propagated from another unit compiled with checks. Of course, it may be necessary to suppress checks because of timing requirements, but any program without checks is vulnerable.

12
Generic units

Generics provide a mechanism by which a program unit may be defined for a class of problems, and specialized to the needs of a particular program by the compiler.

Generics provide a powerful means by which a program may be "factorized" in order to shorten code, and reduce incidence of errors, by avoiding redefining items which appear in several places in the program. Such factorization is familiar both in the case of a procedure, which is defined in one place but used in several places in a program, and in the case of data types, in which a single type definition for a complex object may be used to create instances by variable declarations at many places.

Generic units permit the extension of the factorization to packages with types, data and operations, and provide also for parameterization of the units in respect of the types of object involved in the operations, and the algorithms to be used. In this way program units can be created appropriate for the needs at the point in the program at which instances of the generic units are formed.

a) Generics should not be used in situations in which normal programming methods are equivalent.

In general, a generic package should not be used instead of a record declaration, instances of the generic package being used instead of variables of the record type. However, it should be remembered that, unlike a record, a generic package may contain constant declarations.

b) Use of generic units should be considered, to provide data abstractions required at many points in a program, even if no parameterization is required.

A package with a data structure hidden in its body, and functions and procedures operating on it, provide data abstraction; inclusion of a task to control access can provide protection against simultaneous access from competing tasks. By the use of a generic package, an identical unit, with its operations, may be provided wherever it is needed in the program. The effect is similar to a private data type with associated operations, which permits units in its scope to declare items of the type, and operate on them with the operations provided. However, the latter case forces the calling program to name its instances of the type in the parameter list of the operation. Defining a generic unit imports operations which are directly accessible by name in the local scope.

Examples of different ways of packaging a stack are given in chapter 7. In 7(iii), the package hides a single data structure for a stack. The use of private data types in 7(iv) and 7(v) provides users with a type STACK, from which many stack instances can be generated. However, calls on the stack operations must have the actual stacks as parameters. In the scope of a variable declaration MY_STACK: STACK; the call on the push operation for that stack takes the form:

```
PUSH(X, MY_STACK);
```

In section 7(vi), the package is defined as generic. Multiple instances may be produced, each a separate object, with its own operations. If several exist in the same scope, then they are distinguished by writing, for example:

```
MY_STACK.PUSH(X);
```

In appropriate cases a "use" clause may permit omission of the prefix MY_STACK (see 8.4a).

c) Generic units with type parameters should be used to provide logically equivalent operations on objects of different type.

d) Name overloading should be used for logically equivalent functions and procedures.

If the operations are so completely equivalent that generics are an appropriate tool, then the use of the same name will be appropriate also (see, for example, PUT and GET of LRM Chapter 14). If it does not seem so, then perhaps the use of generics was also inappropriate.

e) To emphasize the parameters and the generic nature of the bodies, the use of some convention involving "commented sugar" should be considered.

The following style of additional comments might be adopted for example:

```
generic
     --(
          type X is private;
          with function F returns X;
     --)
package P is
     ...
end P;

--generic
package body P is
     ...
end P;
```

If such a presentation is adopted, it should be used consistently throughout a program.

f) In writing generic bodies, attribute enquiries should be used as much as possible to generalize the code produced.

The following example provides the effect of a cyclic type, providing operations NEXT and PREVIOUS on any enumeration type.

```
generic
     --(
          type ANY is (<>);
     --)
package CYCLIC is
     function NEXT(X : ANY) return ANY;
     function PREVIOUS(X : ANY) return ANY;
end CYCLIC;
```

```
--generic
package body CYCLIC is
    function NEXT(X : ANY) return ANY is
    begin
        if X = ANY'LAST then
            return = ANY'FIRST;
        else
            return = ANY'SUCC(X);
        end if;
    end NEXT;

    function PREVIOUS(X : ANY) return ANY is
        ...                    -- Body similar to that of NEXT
end CYCLIC;
```

Within the scope of the declarations

```
package CYCLIC_WEEK is new CYCLIC(DAY);
use CYCLIC_WEEK;
```

the operations NEXT and PREVIOUS generate the cycle of the days in the week correctly for all values of today, so, for example:

```
TOMORROW := NEXT(TODAY);
```

g) The use of formal functions and procedures to create logically different behaviour in different instances of the same unit should be avoided.

Procedures and functions may be passed as parameters to replace formal parameters in the declaration of the generic unit. This is justified if the unit is to provide the logically equivalent operation on objects of different types. It may also be used to perform the same operation on different functions: say tabulate or integrate arbitrary functions. It is not justified to create units which behave in a logically different way in external operations.

Consider the following generic definition:

```
generic
    --(
        type X is private;
        with function PLUS(A, B : X) return X;
    --)
function SUM(A, B : X) return X is
begin
    return PLUS(A, B);
end SUM;
```

Correct use of this definition to overload the + operator for new types is

```
function "+" is new SUM
              (X => MATRIX, PLUS => MATRIX_SUM);
function "+" is new SUM
              (X => COMPLEX, PLUS => COMPLEX_ADDITION);
function "+" is new SUM
              (X => SET, PLUS => SET_UNION);
```

It would be bad style, for example, to use this generic to instantiate the function HYPOTENUSE:

```
function HYPOTENUSE is new SUM
              (X => REAL, PLUS => SUMSQ);
```

where SUMSQ evaluates the square root of ($A^2 + B^2$).

h) In general generics should be used only for library units.

i) Only simple forms of generics should be used in application programs.

It should be recognized that general generic definitions are difficult to write correctly. Systems programmers will use more sophisticated forms to provide general library units for use by application programmers.

j) Names for generic objects should be chosen using the same considerations as for types (see 4.1).

A generic definition introduces a class of objects. Names for instances should be more specific, as for variables.

k) Care should be used to avoid misunderstandings due to the reuse of familiar reserved words with different meanings.

The use of "with" to introduce a subprogram parameter is totally different from its use to control visibility (see chapter 10), so is unlikely to cause confusion. The use of "private" and "limited" are dangerously similar to their use with private data types, while being actually different.

1) All considerations for style given in preceding chapters for normal program units apply also to their generic equivalents.

13

Representation clauses and implementation-dependent features

a) Machine-dependent and low level Ada features should be avoided except when absolutely necessary.

Representation clauses, interrupts, machine code inserts, unchecked programming and low level input-output should be avoided. They make programs difficult to understand, prone to errors, and less portable. When essential to use them, their existence, justification and effect must be carefully documented.

Machine code inserts cause problems when trying to interface them with debuggers, when allocating storage, etc.

b) Representation clauses and implementation dependent features should be if possible hidden inside packages which present implementation independent interfaces to users.

This improves program portability (see Portability Guide 13.1).

c) Representation clauses should not be used to change the meaning of a program.

They can be used to affect performance (see rule d below). Address clauses which amount to aliasing should be avoided. Length clauses should not be used that might raise exceptions where no error would occur without the clause.

d) Representation clauses and implementation-dependent features should only be used to increase efficiency, for interrupts, or for interfacing to hardware or foreign code.

They can be used to reduce the run time or storage consumption of a program beyond that which would otherwise be obtained if the compiler were left to its own devices. However the pragmas PACK or OPTIMIZE should be used in preference to representation clauses if sufficient effect is obtained thereby.

They may have to be used to deal with hardware which requires certain information to be in fixed storage positions, e.g. for direct memory access (DMA). The clauses can position the Ada data structures for this. Similarly data may be positioned for interfacing with software in other languages (a problem for some years to come!), e.g. for sharing a 'COMMON' area. Control can be transfered to such software by procedure call (see LRM 13.9).

e) Representation clauses features should be put close to the objects affected.

f) Interrupt routines should be kept as short as possible.

Interrupt routines will be high priority, and should be kept short so as not to cause excessive delay to other processing.

14
Input-output

The requirements for input-output and interrupts will depend very much on the system design, whose style is not addressed as such in this guide. Thus for example the issue of where to put the boundary between hardware and software is not included as such. However if the hardware is regarded as performing some function (in the general sense) then it can be regarded as containing software, and the software partitioning rules of this guide apply.

Input-output can be considered in three different classes, requiring different programming techniques:

(i) Input-output for secondary storage files

(ii) Input-output for the man-machine interface

(iii) Input-output for controlled equipment.

These are discussed under 14.1, 14.3 and 14.6 respectively, to correspond to relevant sections of the LRM. This is not to say that only these sections of the LRM are relevant to these classes of input-output respectively.

14.1 External Files and File Objects

For secondary storage files, two different kinds of actions are performed, namely access (which can be sequential or direct) and management. File management stands not only for such things as file creation and naming, but also for physical actions that may have to be undertaken by the program, e.g. management of multi-volume files.

a) File management software should be encapsulated in packages.

This allows construction of a logical, application-oriented interface between the mass-storage file management software and the rest of the program. An index-sequential-access-mode package would be an example.

b) Non-textual input-output should be controlled by subprogram calls, either to file management packages or to the standard packages.

These calls can be simple and provide a good modelling of secondary storage operation, so they can be used freely in the program text, without specific style conventions. Secondary storage files for text are generally human oriented for display or print-out, and so are discussed under the man-machine class of input-output (see 14.3 below).

14.3 Text Input-Output

The "friendliness" of the man-machine interface is generally more important than the efficiency of implementation of that interface. The amount of processing required to convert information from a form convenient for the human to a form convenient for machine processing, and vice versa, can easily result in the program being cluttered up by input-output formatting.

a) Formatting activities should be grouped into specialized packages with simple interfaces.

Such packages may be application dependent in some cases. The role of these packages is to present:

(i) An interface to the program which is convenient from the programmer's point of view. Such an interface may consist of simple procedure calls for filling in, or displaying, groups of related information, for example records representing the variable part of a screen

(ii) A friendly interface to the user at a terminal, with, for example, immediate detection (and possibly correction) of typing errors, "menu" selection, "help" facility, etc.

b) Input-output on the STANDARD_INPUT and STANDARD_OUTPUT files should use the "long" form of the subprograms of the TEXT_IO package.

The "short" form uses the CURRENT_INPUT and CURRENT_OUTPUT files, which are dynamically, rather than statically, associated with a particular physical file or device.

c) Line and page formatting should be done using the NEW_LINE and NEW_PAGE subprograms, rather than explicitly writing end-of-line or end-of-page characters.

Such characters can have an effect varying from one device to another, and their use frequently results in unreadable and error prone programs. For example

```
NEW_LINE(STANDARD_OUTPUT);
```

is considerably better than

```
PUT(ASCII.CR);
PUT(ASCII.LF);
PUT(ASCII.NUL);
```

which has a somewhat unpredictable effect.

d) Exceptions should be used for dealing with invalid input.

In order to make full use of the options available with the GET procedure, the appropriate option for valid input should be selected and enclosed in a block with an exception handler to deal with invalid input. See, for example, 'GET(SELECTION)' in LRM 14.7.

14.6 Low Level Input-Output

This is designed for operations on physical devices. However if one regards each such device as having a software function, controlled equipment can be treated as a collection of Ada tasks. Input-output can then be seen as calling from the program to the equipment and interrupts as vice versa. It is conceivable to actually implement such calling by rendezvous if an appropriate stub for the equipment function appears in the program.

a) Low level input-output should be encapsulated in task objects associated with each item of controlled equipment.

This rule is associated with the role of tasks to model or control co-existing objects in the problem domain (see Chapter 9). These task objects may themselves be encapsulated in a package or packages, such as to restrict the device dependencies to within the package or packages. This allows the rest of the program to see only the logical properties of the devices.

b) Control should be exercised from the program to the controlled equipment rather than vice versa.

Scanning for input is thus preferred to the interrupt, except when the occasional very fast response is required. Having control from the program is more determinate (see 1.7p).

References and bibliography

The items marked with a "*" are not referenced in the Portability or Style guides.

Abbott, R.J. (1982)
Ada Style Guide (draft)
The Aerospace Corporation, Los Angeles

Abbott, R.J. & Booch, G. (1982)
A Usage Guide for Ada
The Aerospace Corporation, Los Angeles

Adrion, W.R., Branstad, M.A. and Cherniavsky (1982)
Validation, Verification and Testing of Computer Software
ACM Computing Surveys <u>14</u> 2 June 1982

Alagic, S. & Arbib, M.A. (1978) *
The Design of Well-Structured and Correct Programs
Springer-Verlag

ANSI (1983)
Reference Manual for the Ada Programming Language
ANSI/MIL-STD 1815A. Alsys, La Celle-Saint-Cloud, January 1983

Atkinson, L.V. (1979)
Should if...then...else... Follow the Dodo?
Software Practice and Experience <u>9</u> 693-700

Barnes, J.G.P. (1983)
Programming in Ada
Addison-Wesley

Bersoff, E.H., Henderson, V.D. and Siegel, S.G. (1980) *
Software Configuration Management
Prentice-Hall

Bishop, J.M. (1979)
On Publication Pascal
Software Practice and Experience <u>9</u> 711-717

Bjoerner, D. & Jones, C.B. (1982) *
Formal Specification and Software Development
Prentice-Hall

Booch, G. (1982) *
Object-Oriented Design
ACM Ada Letters <u>1</u> I-3.64 - I-3.76

Booch, G. (1983) *
Software Engineering with Ada
Benjamin/Cummings Publishing Co.

Brinch Hansen, P. (1977) *
The Architecture of Concurrent Programs
Prentice-Hall

Buckle, J.K. (1982) *
Software Configuration Management
Macmillan

Clarke, L.A., Wileden, J.C. and Wolf, A.L. (1980)
Nesting in Ada Programs is for the Birds
ACM SIGPLAN Notices 15, 11 139-145

Cohen, N.H. (1982) *
Parallel Quicksort: An Exploration of Concurrent Programming in Ada. ACM Ada Letters 2 II-2.61 - II-2.68

Conway, R. (1978) *
A Primer on Disciplined Programming
Winthrop

Curry, I., (1982)
Separate Compilation in Ada
Ada UK News, November 1982

Dahl, O.-J., Dijkstra, E.W. and Hoare, C.A.R. (1972)
Structured Programming
Academic Press

DeRemer, F. & Kron, H.H. (1976)
Programming-in-the-large versus Programming-in-the-small
IEEE Transactions on Software Engineering 2 80-86, June 1976

Dijkstra, E.W. (1976)
A Discipline of Programming
Prentice-Hall

Downes, V. & Goldsack, S.J. (1982)
Programming Embedded Systems with Ada
Prentice-Hall

Gallaher, L.H. (1982) *
Investigate Capability of Ada for Developing Machine Independent Software. RADC-TR-82-46, Rome Air Development Center, New York

Gardner, M.R., Brubaker, N., Dahlke, C., Goodhart, B. and Ross, D.L. (1983). Ada Programming Style
Intellimac, Inc., Rockville, MD, January 1983.

Gordon, M. (1982)
Byron: a Program Design Language and Document Tool
Intermetrics Ada Update 5, October 1982

Green, T.R.G. (1980) *
Ifs and Thens: Is Nesting just for the Birds
Software Practice and Experience 10 373-381

Gries, D. (1981) *
The Science of Programming
Springer-Verlag

Hansen, D.R. (1981) *
Is Block Structure Necessary?
Software Practice and Experience 11 853-866

Hibbard, P., Hisgen, A., Rosenberg, J., Shaw, M. and Sherman, M. (1981)
Studies in Ada Style
Springer-Verlag

Hueras, J. & Ledgard, H.F. (1977) *
An Automatic Formatting Program for Pascal
ACM SIGPLAN Notices 12 7 82-84

IEEE (1982)
IEEE Standard Glossary of Software Engineering Terminology
IEEE Standard 729-1982. IEEE, New York

Jackson, M.A. (1975)
Principles of Program Design
Academic Press

Jackson, M.A. (1982)
System Development
Prentice-Hall

Jones, C.B. (1980) *
Software Development: A Rigorous Approach
Prentice-Hall

Kernighan, B.W. & Plauger, P.J. (1974a) *
Programming Style: Examples and Counter Examples
ACM Computing Surveys 6 303-319

Kernighan, B.W. & Plauger, P.J. (1974b) *
The Elements of Programming Style
McGraw-Hill

Krieg-Brueckner, B., Luckham, D.C., von Henke, F.W. and Owe, O. (1982)
Draft Reference Manual for Anna, a language for annotating Ada programs. Stanford/ARPA

Ledgard, H.F. (1975) *
Programming Proverbs
Hayden

Ledgard, H.F., Singer, A. and Hueras, J. (1977) *
A Basis for Executing Pascal Programmers
ACM SIGPLAN Notices 12 7 101-105

McGettrick, A. (1982)
Program Verification Using Ada
Cambridge

Mascot (1980)
The Official Handbook of Mascot, December 1980
Mascot Suppliers Association

Mayoh, B. (1982) *
Problem Solving with Ada
Wiley

Meyers, G.J. (1973)
Composite design: the design of modular programs
IBM Technical Report TR-00.2406, IBM Poughkeepsie, January 1973

Meyers, G.J. (1975)
Reliable Software Through Composite Design
Petrocelli/Charter, New York, 1975

Mohilner, P.R. (1978) *
Pretty-printing Pascal Programs
ACM SIGPLAN Notices 13 7 34-40

Nissen, J.C.D., Wichmann, B.A. and others (1982) *
Ada-Europe Guidelines for Ada compiler specification and selection, NPL Report DITC 10/82

Page-Jones, M. (1980)
The Practical Guide to Structured Systems Design
Yourdon Press

Parnas, D.L. (1972a)
A Technique for Software Module Specification with Examples
CACM 15 330-336

Parnas, D.L. (1972b)
On the Criteria to be Used in Decomposing Systems into Modules
CACM 15 1053-1058

Peterson, J.L. (1977) *
On the Formatting of Pascal Programs
ACM SIGPLAN Notices 12 12 83-86

Reynolds, J.C. (1981) *
The Craft of Programming
Prentice-Hall

Sale, A. (1979a)
Pascal Stylistics and Reserved Words
Software Practice and Experience 9 821-825

Sale, A. (1979b)
Miniscules and Majuscules
Software Practice and Experience 9 915-919

Schneider, G.M. & Breull, S.C. (1981) *
Advanced Programming and Problem Solving with Pascal
Wiley

Sherman, M., Hisgen, A. and Rosenberg, J. (1982) *
A Methodology for Programming Abstract Data Types in Ada
Proc ACM AdaTec Conf on Ada, Arlington, October 1982, 66-75

Symm, G.T., Wichmann, B.A., Kok, J. and Winter, D.T. (1983) *
Guidelines for the design of Large Modular Scientific Libraries in Ada. Report DITC 28/83, NPL, July 1983

Taylor, R.N. (1983) *
A General-Purpose Algorithm for Analysing Concurrent Programs
CACM 26 5 362-376, May 1983

Wegner, P. (1980) *
Programming with Ada
Prentice-Hall

Wegner, P. (1983) *
On the Unification of Data and Program Abstraction in Ada
Department of Computer Science, Brown University

Welsh, J. & McKeag, M. (1980) *
Structured System Programming
Prentice-Hall

Wichmann, B.A. (1983)
Tutorial Material on the Real Data Types in Ada
NPL Report to be published

Winterstein, G., Persch, G., Drossopolou, S. and Dausmann, M. (1981) *
Ada Documentation and Programming Guidelines
Bericht Nr 20/81, Inst. fur Informatik, University of Karlsruhe

Wirth, N. (1971) *
Program Development by Stepwise Refinement
CACM 14 221-227

Wirth, N. (1973) *
Systematic Programming
Prentice-Hall

Wirth, N. (1976) *
Algorithms + Data Structures = Programs
Prentice-Hall

Woodward, M.R, (1980)
Experience with Path Analysis and Testing of Programs
IEEE Transactions on Software Engineering, 6, 3, May 1980

Yehudi, A. (1982) *
Data Abstraction: Types versus Objects
ACM Ada Letters 2 II-2.46 - II-2.48

Index

Section references following "Port" refer to the Portability Guide; those following "Style" refer to the Style Guide.